PEARSON

my World GEOGRAPHY

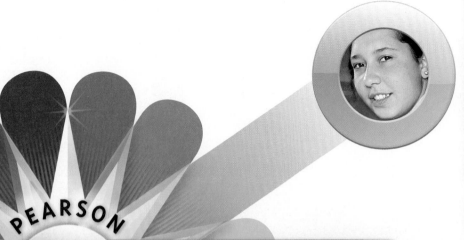

Middle America

Boston, Massachusetts • Chandler, Arizona • Glenview, Illinois • Upper Saddle River, New Jersey

ISBN-13 978-0-13-369772-8
ISBN-10 0-13-369772-X

3 4 5 6 7 8 9 10 **V064** 14 13 12 11 10

Master Teachers and Contributing Authors

George Sabato
Past President, California Council
for the Social Studies
Placerville Union School District
Placerville, California

Michael Yell
Past President, National Council
for the Social Studies
Hudson Middle School
Hudson, Wisconsin

Program Authors

Gregory H. Chu
Professor and Chair of Department
of Geography
University of Wisconsin-La Crosse
La Crosse, Wisconsin

Don Holtgrieve
Department of Planning, Public
Policy, and Management
University of Oregon
Eugene, Oregon

Susan Hardwick
Department of Geography
University of Oregon
Eugene, Oregon

Program Consultant

Grant Wiggins
President of Authentic Education
Hopewell, New Jersey

Teacher Consultants

James F. Dowd IV
Pasadena, California

Susan M. Keane
Rochester Memorial School
Rochester, Massachusetts

Timothy T. Sprain
Lincoln Middle School
La Crosse, Wisconsin

Marilyn Weiser
North Dakota Geographic
Alliance Coordinator
Minot State University
Minot, North Dakota

CONTENTS

Middle America

Carolina, from
Mexico ▼

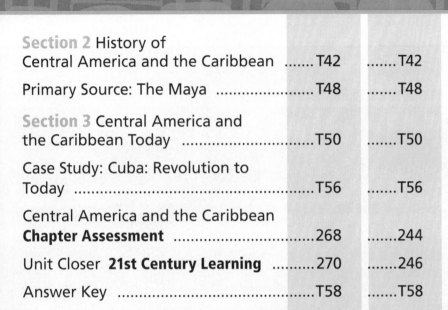

Luis, from the Dominican
Republic in the Caribbean ▶

Middle America

- Prepare to learn about Middle America and activate prior knowledge by creating KWL (Know, Want to know, Learned) tables, filling out only the K and W columns. Correct any misconceptions or misinformation in the tables.

- Have students preview maps, photos, and other visuals and predict what they will learn about Middle America.

GUIDE ON THE SIDE

What time is it there? Have students look at the time zone display to determine by how many hours the times in Washington, D.C. and Mexico City differ. (1 hour)

Analyze Maps Point out the political map and have students answer the following questions.

- Which Middle American country is the largest? (Mexico)

- Which country lies farthest south? (Panama)

- What is the capital of Mexico? (Mexico City)

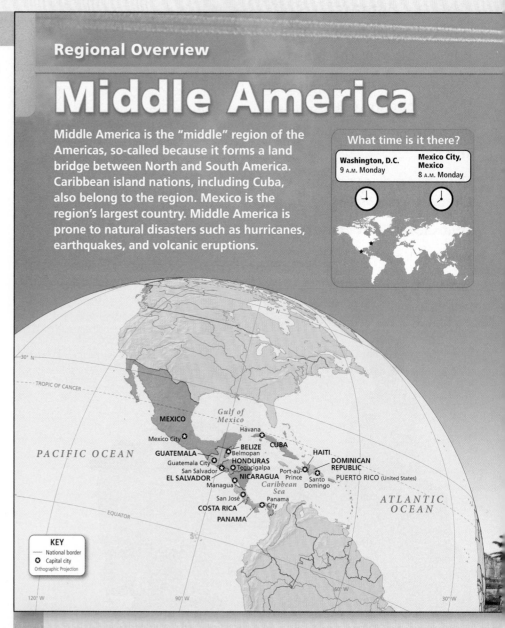

Regional Overview

Middle America

Middle America is the "middle" region of the Americas, so-called because it forms a land bridge between North and South America. Caribbean island nations, including Cuba, also belong to the region. Mexico is the region's largest country. Middle America is prone to natural disasters such as hurricanes, earthquakes, and volcanic eruptions.

What time is it there?

Washington, D.C.	Mexico City, Mexico
9 A.M. Monday	8 A.M. Monday

MEXICO
Mexico City
Gulf of Mexico
Havana
CUBA
BELIZE
GUATEMALA
Belmopan
HONDURAS
Guatemala City
Tegucigalpa
HAITI
San Salvador
Port-au-Prince
DOMINICAN REPUBLIC
EL SALVADOR
NICARAGUA
Santo Domingo
PUERTO RICO (United States)
Managua
Caribbean Sea
PACIFIC OCEAN
San José
Panama City
ATLANTIC OCEAN
COSTA RICA
PANAMA

KEY
— National border
✪ Capital city
Orthographic Projection

THE UNIT AHEAD

In this unit, students will

- study the geography of Middle America.
- get to know teenagers from Mexico and the Dominican Republic.
- go On Assignment in Mexico, Central America, and the Caribbean.

- make connections among the physical geography, history, politics, and culture of Middle America.

The Unit Ahead

➡ **Chapter 3** Mexico

➡ **Chapter 4** Central America and the Caribbean

my worldgeography.com

Plan your trip online by doing a Data Discovery Activity and watching the myStory Videos of the region's teens.

my Story

Carolina
Age: 16
Home: Tamaulipas, Mexico
Chapter 3

my Story

Luis
Age: 17
Home: Limón, Dominican Republic
Chapter 4

The Mayan ruins of Tulum, south of Cancun on the Yucatán Peninsula

GUIDE ON THE SIDE

my Story

Make Predictions Make predictions about the teen students you will get to know in this unit.

- Carolina is 16 and Luis is 17. Do you think they work, go to school, or both? Explain why you think so. (Sample: Yes, I think they work and study because some of the teenagers I know got jobs once they were in high school.)

- Find Luis's country on the globe. Based on its location, what would you guess its climate is like? (warm or tropical)

NOTES

GEOGRAPHY

Mexico's Rain Forest The Mexican rain forest, along with lowland rain forests in Belize and Guatemala, was once the northernmost area of the Amazon rain forest. Home to jaguars, howler monkeys, macaws, and other native species, Mexico's rain forest is richly diverse. Nevertheless, human activity has had a serious impact on this ecosystem, causing the rain forest to shrink to about thirty percent of its former size. The cutting of trees for pastureland, as well as poaching, illegal logging, and oil exploration, have all taken their toll, causing many plant and animal species to become extinct.

In recent years, however, the Mexican government has put measures in place to preserve this fragile natural resource. As part of the Mesoamerican Biological Corridor project, Mexico is working to connect protected rain forests in Middle America so that wildlife may move freely between them.

Analyze Visuals Ask students to look at the labeled satellite photo, which shows key physical patterns in the region.

- To what group of Caribbean islands does Cuba belong? (the Greater Antilles)

- What type of landform makes up most of Middle America? (an isthmus)

- Which mountain range lies east of Mexico's central plateau? (the Sierra Madre Oriental)

- What is the name of Mexico's western peninsula? (Baja California)

Regional Overview
Physical Geography

The Sierra Madre ranges lie near both of Mexico's coasts.

Baja California

Gulf of California

Sierra Madre Occidental

Mexican Plateau

Sierra Madre Oriental

Gulf of Mexico

Yucatán Peninsula

Greater

Caribbean

PACIFIC OCEAN

Southern Mexico's rain forest supports diverse animal and plant life.

Active volcanoes dot the west coast of Nicaragua.

COMMON MISCONCEPTIONS

Baja California Many people think that Baja California is part of the United States. This is an understandable mistake, since the peninsula's name, "lower California," seems to refer to California, one of the fifty United States. Nevertheless, Baja California belongs to Mexico.

A peninsula some 760 miles long, Baja California is shared by two Mexican States. The northern state,

Baja California, has the same name as the peninsula. Its capital, Mexicali, lies close to the U.S. border town of Calexico. The southern state is Baja California Sur. Its capital city of La Paz is located close to the peninsula's southern tip. Many luxury resorts populate the southern area called Los Cabos. In 1973 the completion of the Transpeninsular Highway greatly facilitated travel from one end of the peninsula to the other.

Cuba is the largest island in the Caribbean Sea. It belongs to a group of islands called the Greater Antilles.

ATLANTIC OCEAN

Lesser Antilles

Antilles Sea

Regional Flyover

Suppose you are flying in an airplane across Middle America. If you begin in the north and fly southeast, you would fly over the Sierra Madre Occidental mountain range in Mexico. Mexico's central plateau and the second range of the Sierra Madres are both to the east. As you continue flying south, you would see the lush vegetation of lower Mexico's rain forests.

East of Mexico is the Caribbean Sea and its many islands. Cuba, Jamaica, Puerto Rico, and Hispaniola, which includes both Haiti and the Dominican Republic, are part of the Greater Antilles. The Virgin Islands, Antigua, and other smaller islands make up the Lesser Antilles.

Your flight turns southwest over Central America. Soon you notice an isthmus, or a narrow land bridge between two larger land masses. The isthmus includes Costa Rica and Panama, the southernmost country of Middle America, where your flight ends.

➲ **In-Flight Movie**
Take flight over Middle America and explore the region from the air.

Regional Flyover

Analyze Visuals Read Regional Flyover and ask the following questions about the labeled satellite photo.

- Look at Hispaniola, the second-largest Caribbean island. What is different about its eastern and western halves? (The eastern half is greener.)

- Which peninsula forms part of eastern Mexico? (the Yucatan Peninsula)

- Which body of water lies directly east of Mexico? Directly east of Central America? (the Gulf of Mexico; the Caribbean Sea)

- Why do you think the region attracts many tourists? (It has a warm climate and extensive coastal areas.)

➲ **Inflight Movie**

Before playing the Inflight Movie, ask,
- What might be visible from the air but not from the ground?
- What landforms might you see?
- How does this information help you understand the region's geography?

NOTES

ECONOMICS

Struggling Economies Most countries in Middle America have struggling economies. This is due to a combination of factors, including political unrest and natural disasters such as earthquakes, hurricanes, and volcanic eruptions. While a number of countries are benefiting from growing tourism industries, they face the challenge of preserving natural areas visited by large numbers of tourists.

Free trade agreements have increased trade but have also created some new economic challenges. In Mexico, for example, increased manufacturing has provided more jobs. At the same time, many Mexican farmers find it difficult to compete with imported agricultural products. Unable to support their families, many leave the region to find work abroad. Those who succeed send money home to their families.

GUIDE ON THE SIDE

Middle America's Economy

Analyze Visuals Point out the images showing various economic activities in Middle America.

- Which images most represent aspects of trade? Explain. (the factory worker, who may be producing goods for export, and the Panama Canal, which was built to facilitate the shipping of goods)

- Do you think the farmer is likely to engage in trade? Why or why not? Explain. (Probably not, because crops produced manually are not likely to yield a surplus.)

- What environmental concern might be associated with ecotourism? (the need to respect and preserve the natural environment)

Regional Geography
Human Geography

Middle America's Economy

People who live in Middle America have a variety of jobs. In countries such as Haiti, the majority of people farm for a living. In Mexico, many people work in factories that manufacture goods for export, or for sale in other countries. In Central America and the Caribbean, many people work in the region's thriving tourism industry.

Despite the variety of economic activities, many people in this region are poor. Natural disasters, such as hurricanes, continually cause economic setbacks. Some people emigrate, or move to other countries. Many immigrants who find work in the United States send money to family members back home.

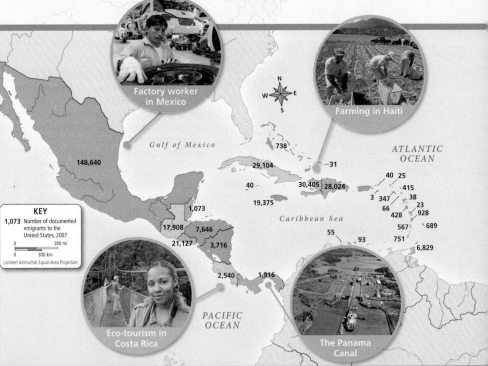

KEY

1,073 Number of documented emigrants to the United States, 2007

0 — 300 mi
0 — 300 km
Lambert Azimuthal Equal-Area Projection

Factory worker in Mexico

Farming in Haiti

Eco-tourism in Costa Rica

The Panama Canal

Gulf of Mexico

ATLANTIC OCEAN

Caribbean Sea

PACIFIC OCEAN

148,640
29,104
40
19,375
1,073
17,908 7,646
21,127 3,716
2,540 1,916
738
31
30,405 28,024
40 25
415
3 347 38
66 428 23 928
567 689
55 93 751
6,829

PRIMARY SOURCE

Poverty Referring to the Haitian people, Hedi Annabi, representative to the U.N. Secretary General, observed, "[P]eople who are hungry have no stake in stability." —Morning Edition, April 18, 2008, National Public Radio

One of the world's poorest countries, Haiti experienced food riots in the spring of 2008. Although two thirds of Haiti's people are employed in agriculture, many Haitians do not have enough to eat. Contributing factors to the lack of food include deforestation, extensive damage from hurricanes, and inflated food prices. Although the cost of food declined somewhat in 2009, food is still unaffordable for most Haitians, 80 percent of whom live on about $2 per day. Factors contributing to the global inflation of food prices include drought and the diversion of corn and soybeans to biofuel production.

my World IN NUMBERS

	Mexico	Honduras	Costa Rica	Haiti
Literacy rate (15 years of age or older)	91.0%	80.0%	94.9%	52.9%
Income earned by wealthiest 10% of population	37.1%	42.2%	37.4%	47.70%
Urban population**	75.0%	46.0%	61.0%	37.0%
People employed in agriculture	15.1%	39.2%	14.0%	66.0%

SOURCE: CIA World Factbook Online, 2009
** SOURCE: Population Division of the United Nations Secretariat, 2003

Put It Together

1. What are two of Mexico's main physical features?

2. What type of natural disasters frequently occur in Middle America?

3. Compare Mexico and Haiti. What is the relationship between the percentage of urban population and the percentage of people employed in agriculture?

 Data Discovery

Find your own data to make a regional data table.

Size Comparison

The United States is about twice as big as Middle America.

---

myWorld in Numbers

Analyze Visuals Point out the chart and use the questions below to help students analyze the data and draw conclusions.

- Which two countries have the highest urban share of population? (Mexico, Costa Rica)

- Is there a relationship between the percent of people employed in agriculture and urban population? Explain. (Yes. Countries with the highest percentage of urban dwellers have the lowest percentage of farm workers.)

- In which country is income distributed most equally? (Mexico) Most unequally? (Haiti)

Data Discovery

Students can practice table and graph skills online with the Data Discovery features on Middle America. They can use their trackers to save data for their On Assignment stories later in the unit.

Plan With Understanding by Design

Chapter Objectives
Begin With the End in Mind

Students will demonstrate the following enduring understandings:
- Geography has a significant effect on settlement patterns.
- The availability of natural resources may not guarantee a country's economic success.
- While diversity may create conflict, it can also enrich a country's culture.

Connect
Make Learning Meaningful

Student Edition
- **Essential Question** How much does geography shape a country?
- **myStory** Carolina spends her weeks at boarding school and her weekends on the farm with her family.

my worldgeography.com
myStory Video Get to know Carolina through a video of her life at home and at school.

Student Journal
Essential Question Preview

Experience
Teach Knowledge and Skills

Student Edition
- Read Sections 1, 2, and 3.
- Answer Reading Checks and Section Assessment questions.

my worldgeography.com
On Assignment Visual Glossary, Active Atlas, Data Discovery, Timeline, and Culture Close-up

Student Journal
- Sections 1, 2, and 3 Word Wise
- Sections 1, 2, and 3 Take Notes

Teacher's Edition
MyWorld Activities
- Section 1: Mexico Goes Global, p. T10
- Section 2: To Dig or Not to Dig, p. T18
- Section 3: Get a Job, p. T26

21st Century Learning Online Tutor
- Read Special-Purpose Maps
- Synthesize
- Analyze Cause and Effect
- Make Decisions
- Identify Main Ideas and Details
- Compare and Contrast

Understand
Assess Understanding

Assessment Booklet
- Chapter Tests   • Benchmark Tests

Teacher's Edition
myWorld Chapter Activity
Students write brief profiles of Mexican leaders and then decide who had the greatest effect on Mexico's history.

Student Journal
Essential Question Writer's Workshop

my worldgeography.com
On Assignment Students submit an online article or a slideshow about how geography has shaped Mexico.

Success Tracker™
Online at myworldgeography.com
Administer chapter tests and remediate understanding.

Student Edition
Chapter Assessment

Connect to the Essential Question

Essential Question

How much does geography shape a country?

Use the Essential Question poster and follow these steps to help students understand the Essential Question.

Connect to Their Lives

1. Have students discuss how they think geography has shaped their lives. (If students have already studied this Essential Question, encourage them to note changes to their opinion.) As students respond, emphasize the diversity of ways that geography can shape their lives. Students might focus on parks, local weather, crops grown in their region, and recreational activities. Ask, Have you ever lived in a place that had different geographic influences? Explain.

2. Have students identify how geographic elements mentioned in the table below have affected their lives. Post the following table for them to complete or have students turn to the *Essential Question Preview* page in their **Student Journal.**

Personal Influence of Geographic Elements				
Parks, Lakes, Rivers	Local Weather	Local Crops	Size of School	Recreational Activities

3. Discuss students' responses. Ask, In what ways can these elements affect each other? For example, how can cold weather affect recreational activities of a region?

Connect to the Content

4. Now have students brainstorm ways in which geographic elements can influence a country. For instance, the amount of rainfall can affect what crops are grown.

5. In the table below, have students list possible influences of geographic elements on a country.

Influences of Geographic Elements on a Country				
Physical Features	Climate	Natural Resources	Population	Culture

6. After previewing the chapter, have students make chapter-related predictions on the *Essential Question Preview* page in the **Student Journal.**

7. Remind students that they will answer a prompt related to the Essential Question on each section's *Take Notes* page in the **Student Journal.**

Explore my worldgeography.com

Welcome to myWorldGeography

http://www.myworldgeography.com

ON ASSIGNMENT: Mexico

For this chapter's assignment, students will
- take a digital trip to Mexico.
- take on the role of a journalist.
- gather notes, images, and data for their story.
- write an article or create a multimedia slideshow connecting the information and images gathered during their trip and this chapter's Essential Question, *How much does geography shape a country?*

ITINERARY

During their trip, students will make the following stops:

 myStory Video

Learn from Carolina about Mazahua culture.

 Active Atlas

Read political, climate, and population maps of Mexico.

 Data Discovery

Gather data from tables and graphs.

 Timeline

Read more about Mexico's historic events.

 Culture Close-up

Discover more about Mexican culture.

 Self-Test

Assess their own knowledge of chapter content.

While on their trip, students will practice the following skills:

- **Interpret** the effects of climate on Mexico's economy.
- **Sequence** important events in Mexico's history.

TakingITGlobal for Educators

Extend the reach of every lesson by helping students connect to a global community of young people with common interests and concerns. Visit myworldgeography.com to
- explore Country Pages relating to Mexico.
- delve deeper into this chapter's Essential Question, *How much does geography shape a country?*
- find online alternatives to and solutions for the Unit Closer 21st Century Learning Activity.

 worldgeography.com

TEACHER CENTER

Preview and assign student materials, enrich your teaching, and track student progress with the following resources:
- Online Lesson Planning and Resource Library
- Presentations for Projection
- Online Teacher's Edition and Ancillaries
- Google Earth Links

Assess Enduring Understandings

| myWorld Chapter Activity | **Step-by-Step Instructions** | 60 min |

A Time for Judgment

Teach this activity at the end of the chapter to assess enduring understandings.

OBJECTIVES

Students will demonstrate the following enduring understandings:
- Geography has a significant effect on settlement patterns.
- The availability of natural resources may not guarantee a country's economic success.
- While diversity may create conflict, it can also enrich a country's culture.

Students will provide the following evidence of understanding:
- Leader Profiles
- Statement of Effect

LEARNING STYLES
- Verbal
- Logical
- Interpersonal

MATERIALS
- Activity Support: Student Instructions and Rubric, p. T6
- Activity Support: Leader's Profile, p. T7
- Activity Cards: #13–18
  - 13. Montezuma
  - 14. Cortés
  - 15. Maximilian
  - 16. Juárez
  - 17. Zapata
  - 18. Calderón

Activity Steps

1. **Set Expectations** Tell the students that it is time for Mexico's leaders to face the judgment of history—and this class's students are the judges.

2. Organize students in teams to create a profile of one of six key leaders of Mexico. Distribute one Activity Card to each team. Utilizing the information they collect from the Activity Cards, teams will judge whether their leader met his goals and how the leader's success or failure has affected Mexican history. Also provide each team with six copies of *Activity Support Leader's Profile*, or have them use extra sheets of paper for five of the profiles.

3. Allow ten minutes for teams to read the Activity Card for their assigned leader and use this historical and biographical information data to complete *Activity Support: Leader's Profile* for that person.

   L3 On-Level Explain that a profile is a document that summarizes key information about someone's life. Tell students it is a very brief biography. If possible, show an example and compare it to a book-length biography.

4. Have students jigsaw to form new teams with one student who can share details about each leader. Have students teach each other about their leader's data, successes, and failures. Students should complete *Activity Support: Leader's Profile* for each leader.

5. Next, ask students to make a judgment as to the level of success each leader had in achieving his goals for Mexico.

   L2 Extra Support Post a simple cause-and-effect diagram on the board for use in assessing a leader's effect on Mexico's history.

6. Direct students to individually write statements declaring which leader's success or failure had the greatest effect on the history of Mexico.

   ELL Intermediate Write this sentence on the board as a model topic sentence for use in writing statements. _____ *had the greatest influence on Mexico's history because he* _____.

   L4 Challenge Have students poll the class to determine which two leaders were chosen by the greatest number of students. Have volunteers debate the merits of each.

| KEY | Time | Individual | Pairs | Small Group | Whole Class |

Name _____ Class _____ Date _____

myWorld Chapter Activity Support   **Student Instructions and Rubric**

A Time for Judgment

Activity Instructions Read the following summary of your myWorld Chapter Activity. Follow your teacher's directions for more information.

1. Read the Activity Card with historical and biographical information about one of six leaders of Mexico: Montezuma II, Cortés, Maximilian I, Juárez, Zapata, Calderón.

2. Working with a team, complete the Activity Support profile for that leader. Then change teams and share information to complete the profiles of the remaining five leaders. Be sure to include the leader's name, information about his early life, key achievements, use of Mexico's resources, and his goal for Mexico.

3. Discuss with your team the effects of each leader's successes and failures.

4. Working independently, write a statement telling which leader you think had the greatest effect on Mexican history.

myWorld Chapter Activity Rubric	3 Exceeds Understanding	2 Reaches Understanding	1 Approaches Understanding
Profile Data	Profile information is complete, detailed, and accurate.	Profile information is complete, includes some details, and is mostly accurate.	Profile information is mostly complete, has few details, and includes several errors.
Leader Statement	Supports statement's position with detailed, factual evidence from Mexico's history	Supports statement's position with factual evidence from Mexico's history	Supports statement's position with little or no evidence from Mexico's history

Name _____ Class _____ Date _____

 myWorld Chapter Activity Support   Leader's Profile

A Time for Judgment

Directions Read the historical and biographical information on your team's Activity Card. Use that information and the table below to complete a profile of the leader described. Exchange information with the other team until you have completed profiles for all six leaders. Use separate sheets of paper for additional profiles. Then on additional sheets of lined paper, write your opinion of which leader had the greatest effect on Mexico's history. Support your opinion with facts.

Leader's Profile

Leader's Name	
Early Life	
Key Achievements	
Use of Mexico's Resources	
Goals for Mexico	
Successes	
Failures	
Effect on Mexico's History	

Mexico

- Introduce the Essential Question so that students will be able to understand the big ideas of this chapter (see earlier page, Connect to the Essential Question).

- Help students prepare to learn about Mexico by looking at the chapter's maps, charts, and photos.

- Have students make and record chapter predictions with the *Essential Question Preview* in the **Student Journal.**

- Ask them to analyze maps on this page.

Explore the Essential Question . . .

Have students complete the Essential Question Writer's Workshop in their **Student Journal** to demonstrate in-depth understanding of the question in the context of this chapter.

Analyze Maps Point out the political map.

- What is the capital of Mexico? (Mexico City)

- Which river forms part of the U.S.-Mexican border? (the Rio Grande)

- In which area of Mexico are most of its cities located? (the central area)

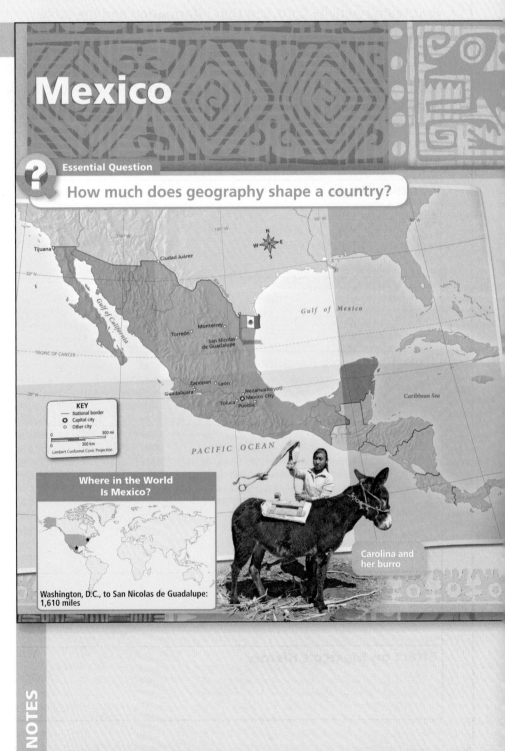

Mexico

Essential Question

How much does geography shape a country?

Where in the World Is Mexico?

Washington, D.C., to San Nicolas de Guadalupe: 1,610 miles

Carolina and her burro

KEY
— National border
⊕ Capital city
○ Other city

NOTES

INTRODUCE  my Story

Get students excited to learn about Mexico by first experiencing the region through the eyes of Carolina, a young woman balancing her family's rural life with her studies and hopes for the future.

- Read myStory and watch the myStory Video about her life.
- Have students complete *A Long Way from Home* in the **Student Journal** to prepare to learn about different communities in the region.

my Story
A Long Way from Home

In this section you'll read about Carolina, a young woman from Mexico's state of Tamaulipas. What does Carolina's story tell you about life in Mexico?

? Explore the Essential Question
- at **my worldgeography.com**
- using the **myWorld Chapter Activity**
- with the **Student Journal**

Story by Monica Maristain for myWorld Geography Online

During the week, Carolina rises early every day, as breakfast is served promptly at 6:30 A.M. Carolina attends Technical High School #1 in Solis, Mexico. She shares a room in a boarding house with three other girls. It hasn't been easy. Carolina's family could not pay for her to attend the school, but through hard work she was able get a scholarship that made it possible. Carolina will be the first in her family to finish her high school and preparatory school studies. "I have seen how my sisters who did not study live, and I do not want that type of life for myself," she says.

After school Carolina works in the school's computer lab until 6 P.M. and then attends a study session until 8 P.M. After dinner at 8 P.M., there is time to spend with her three roommates, or finish up any homework that still needs to be done. "We are supposed to be in bed by 10 P.M.," Carolina laughs, "but often we are still awake when they come by at 11 P.M. to check on us and turn off the lights."

Carolina knows if she wants to go to a university and get a degree she has to get good grades in school and get another scholarship. Carolina hopes to study medicine or communications in college. "Among my family and in my community there aren't too many professionals."

GUIDE ON THE SIDE

my Story

A Long Way from Home

- **Identify Details** Where does Carolina live during the week? (in a boarding house near her school)
- **Cause and Effect** What made it possible for Carolina to go to high school? (She worked hard to earn a scholarship.)
- **Compare and Contrast** How will high school graduation set Carolina apart from the rest of her family? (She will be the first to complete high school.)

→ **On Assignment**

Have students go to myworldgeography.com to receive their assignments from a virtual newspaper editor. Students will explore Mexico to better understand Carolina's story and the key ideas of the chapter.

NOTES

CORE CONCEPTS: WHAT IS CULTURE?

Review Core Concept 7.1 before discussing with your students the Mazahua culture and Carolina's view of it. Discuss the definitions of *culture* and *cultural region*. Ask students to predict whether Mexico has more than one cultural region. Then have students read to identify cultural traits of the Mazahua.

Have students also read to answer the following questions: What aspects of the Mazahua culture does Carolina value? In what ways is she departing from her family's way of life to prepare for her future?

With friends at school

Eating at home

Analyze Visuals Point out and discuss the images on both pages.

- Which images show Carolina during a weekend? Explain. (her family, eating at home, shopping for food; during the week she is away at school)

- What similarities do you see between Carolina's life and that of American students? (She goes to school, spends time with friends and family, and rides her bike.)

- **Cause and Effect** Why does Carolina plan to attend a university? (to have a better future)

- **Summarize** What kind of town is San Nicolas de Guadalupe? (a farming community whose people are friendly)

Carolina admits, "that is what I wish for the most... to get my diploma and to have a better future."

Each weekend Carolina travels by bus for three hours back to her home town. Along the way, she talks about how very different her life is at home. "San Nicolas de Guadalupe is a farming community full of hayfields and animals and plenty of dirt and dust," she says.

Fortunately, there are many other things that Carolina loves about her home. "The people there are very friendly," Carolina says. "When we have celebrations, everyone helps with the preparation of food and other things that need to be done."

Carolina, like most of the people in her home town, is one of the Mazahua, an indigenous group. Carolina can speak her native language in addition to Spanish, but many young people cannot. "I have cousins and if I speak to them in Mazahua, they sit there thinking, 'What did she say?' They say

Back home in San Nicholas de Guadalupe, Carolina visits a market to get ingredients for dinner. On the right, a clay table and roller are used in making tortillas.

ECONOMICS

Economic Diversity Many Mazahua work as laborers on area farms or cattle ranches, while others work in factories. Some move to cities to work in construction or as housekeepers. Nevertheless, traditional crafts still contribute to the economy. Roots of the zacatón, a plant that grows in the region, are used to make brushes and brooms. Other crafts include the making of baskets, pottery, and textiles. There is often a division of labor, with each family member performing a specific task to produce a particular product. For example, women decorate clay pottery that is then fired by the men.

To increase profitability, those who produce crafts often form cooperatives. Similarly, families raise crops on land that is shared.

Carolina's family in San Nicholas de Guadalupe

Carolina on her way to the cyber cafe

that they should not speak Mazahua, because they will not be accepted at school or because speaking Mazahua is something bad." Carolina is very concerned that if her people's native language is lost it will not be long before her entire culture vanishes. "So much is already being lost. Only the older women still dress in the traditional way."

It is already dark by the time Carolina steps off the bus in San Nicolas de Guadalupe and there is little left to do but have dinner and head off to bed for some much-deserved rest.

Carolina's weekends at home are spent doing household chores or helping in the fields, but usually she finds some time for fun. One of her favorite activities is riding her bike. She also likes to do traditional Mazahua crafts such as embroidery and knitting. Then, of course, there are Mazahua festivals. "I like to dance," Carolina says. "The cumbia (a dance from Colombia) and the quebradita, which is a Mexican version of the cumbia—at my house we dance to everything!"

As the music plays in the background and the sun sets on another weekend in San Nicolas de Guadalupe, Carolina finally gets a chance to sit back and enjoy the moment. Tomorrow morning as she boards the bus back to school, she won't be leaving this all behind. . .she'll be taking it with her into the future.

myStory Online

Join Carolina as she shows you more about her life in San Nicolas de Guadalupe.

Meet the Journalist

Name David House
Favorite Moment Spending time with Carolina's warm, welcoming family

NOTES

- **Cause and Effect** Why does Carolina feel it is important to speak Mazahua? (She wants to preserve her native culture.)

- **Identify Details** How does Carolina help out at home? (by doing household chores or helping in the fields)

- **Summarize** What other aspects of Mazahua culture does Carolina enjoy? (embroidery, knitting, festivals)

 myStory Video

Have students watch the video at myworldgeography.com about Carolina's life at school and at home.

Chapter Atlas

OBJECTIVES

Students will know

- Mexico's seven landform regions.
- the effects of climate on agriculture in various regions.

Students will be able to

- identify and locate major physical and political features of the region on a map.
- describe the effects of human activity on the environment.

SET EXPECTATIONS

In this section, students will

- read Chapter Atlas.
- summarize the economic potential of Mexico's natural resources.
- go On Assignment in Mexico and learn more about the climate where Carolina lives.

CORE CONCEPTS

You may wish to teach or reteach the following lessons from the Core Concepts Handbook:

- Temperature, pp. 34–35
- People's Impact on the Environment, pp. 52–53
- Population Growth, pp. 74–75

KEY

Differentiated Instruction
L1 Special Needs **L2** Extra Support
L3 On-Level **L4** Challenge

English Language Instruction
ELL Beginner **ELL** Early Intermediate **ELL** Intermediate
ELL Early Advanced **ELL** Advanced

1 Connect
Make learning meaningful

Make Connections Have students think about oil and other natural resources that generate energy. Give students five minutes to write down everything they did so far today that required oil, gas, or electricity. If they know which form of energy they used for each task, ask them to write that down as well. Discuss how depletion of these resources would affect their lives.

ELL **Beginner/Early Intermediate** Show or draw images of tasks and items that a lack of energy resources would affect, such as a light bulb or a car.

Activate Prior Knowledge Ask students what they already know about the climate and landforms of Mexico, possibly from books, cartoons, or television shows. Ask them to predict whether the climate would be the same in every part of Mexico.

L2 **Extra Support** Use an outline map to show the shared border of the United States and Mexico. Ask, Is the climate the same all over the United States? If not, would it be the same in all of Mexico? Explain why or why not.

Prepare Follow the steps in the section **Preview.** Preteach the Key Terms. Then have students complete *Word Wise* in their journals using in-text clues and the glossary for help.

2 Experience
Teach knowledge and skills

Read Use **Background** notes and **Guide on the Side** questions to model active reading. Have students use *Take Notes* in their **Student Journal** to record important places to know in Mexico on an outline map. Students should use the maps in the Chapter Atlas and the Active Atlas at myworldgeography.com for assistance.

ELL **Intermediate** Have Spanish speakers scan the section maps for Spanish terms and names, such as *Sierra* and *Baja*, and then use a dictionary to translate them into English. Invite students to pronounce terms they identify and share translations with the class.

L1 **Special Needs** Have students read the **Online Student Edition** while listening to the accompanying audio.

L4 **Challenge** Have students read *Enrichment: A Slowly Sinking City* to learn about people's negative impact on the environment in Mexico City.

 Practice: myWorld Activity Students will choose a natural resource to develop and export. **Step-by-Step Instructions** and **More Activities** follow on p. T10.

SECTION 1 RESOURCE GUIDE

FOR THE STUDENT

my worldgeography.com Student Center

- Active Atlas
- Data Discovery

Student Edition (print and online)

- Chapter Atlas

Student Journal (print and online)

- Section 1 Word Wise
- Section 1 Take Notes

21st Century Learning Online Tutor

- Read Special-Purpose Maps
- Synthesize

FOR THE TEACHER

my worldgeography.com Teacher Center

- Online Lesson Planner
- Presentations for Projection
- SuccessTracker

ProGuide: Middle America

- Section 1 Lesson Plan, pp. T8–T9
- 🚶 myWorld Activity Step-by-Step Instructions, p. T10
- Activity Support: Resource Analysis, p. T11
- myWorld Geography Enrichment, p. T12
- Section Quiz, p. T13

Accelerating the Progress of ELLs

- Comprehension Check Strategies, p. 53

---

3 Understand
Assess understanding

Review Review *Word Wise* and *Take Notes* in the **Student Journal.**

Assess Knowledge and Skills Use the Section Assessment and Section Quiz to check students' progress.

Assess Understanding Review students' responses to the Section Assessment Essential Question prompt.

Remediate Use these strategies to review and remediate.

If students struggle to . . .	Try these strategies.
Recognize Mexico's landforms	Help students identify each on a map.
Describe the impact of human activity on Mexico's environment	Compare images of Mexico before industrialization to contemporary images in the chapter.
Comprehend hydroelectric power	Break *hydroelectric* into two parts, *hydro-* and *electric.*

ELL Support

ELL Objective Students will be able to use English to identify natural resources.

Cultural Connections Have students draw and label bilingually one or more elements of physical geography that are characteristic of their family's home country. Help them to compare what they have drawn to elements of Mexico's physical geography.

ELL Early Intermediate Content Tip To help students identify resources, make flash cards with a visual, such as a simple drawing of an oil well, on one side and the name of the resource on the other. Have students use the cards in pairs to practice identifying resources.

ELL Activity Have students make and play a memory game with printed images of natural resources on one half of the cards and the matching English terms on the others. **(Visual/Kinesthetic)**

myWorld Activity   **Step-by-Step Instructions**

 30 min

Mexico Goes Global

OBJECTIVES

Students will

- play the part of a business tycoon who runs a global conglomerate.
- identify the location of natural resources and explore their industrial potential.

LEARNING STYLE

- Verbal

21st Century Learning

- Synthesize

MATERIALS

- Activity Support: Resource Analysis, p. T11

Activity Steps

1. Tell students they will be role-playing the owner of Global Conglomerates, a very large company that plans to establish an industry in Mexico utilizing a natural resource there.

2. Have students refer to the maps of Mexico's natural resources, population, and the physical map in their texts. Discuss population as a factor in developing natural resources.

3. Students are to examine the the maps in order to identify three locations with resources that have potential for industrial development.

   ELL **Beginning/Early Intermediate** Provide a word bank with visuals of important natural resources in Mexico. Review meanings and pronunciation.

4. Pass out *Activity Support: Resource Analysis* and have students complete the table with information about three potential locations.

5. Tell the students they should select a final location and resource for Global Conglomerates' newest industry and list their reasons on *Activity Support*.

   L2 **Extra Support** Point out bodies of water on the maps. Discuss reasons why water access is important for choosing a site.

6. Have students share their decision and explain their reasons, using the final lines on *Activity Support* to draft ideas. Guide students' thinking with questions: How can you access local and global markets? What kind of transportation is available? What energy resources exist? Where will workers come from?

 More Activities From myWorld Teachers

Local Connections Have students discuss how an increase in the price of oil affects students, their families, and the region in which they live. Then have them discuss how the same increase might affect Mexico, a country dependent on oil for income. **(Verbal)**

Travel Brochure Have students make a travel brochure highlighting features of Mexico's landforms. As an alternative, groups of students could design brochures for a tour agency that brings tourists to one of the landforms. **(Verbal/Visual)**

Rate Regions Have students rate each of Mexico's regions according to its positive and/or negative physical features and conditions, such as desert or mineral-rich. Discuss how the conditions might affect life in each region. **(Logical)**

 my **worldgeography.com**   **Teacher Center**   →   Find additional resources in the online Teacher Center.

Name _____ Class _____ Date _____

myWorld Activity Support   **Resource Analysis**

Mexico Goes Global

Directions Imagine you are the owner of Global Conglomerates, who wishes to establish a new industrial site in Mexico utilizing local resources. Review the maps of Mexico's natural resources and population. List three locations for potential development.

Location	Resource	Industrial Potential

After reviewing the three possible sites, select one location for industrial development. List your specific reasons based on the information you found on the maps. Reasons may include the location's access to local and global markets, transportation and energy, and people available to work in the region. Then draft ideas for an explanation of your decisions.

Location _____

Reasons for Selection _____

_____

_____

_____

Ideas for Explanation _____

_____

_____

_____

Name _____ Class _____ Date _____

Enrichment: A Slowly Sinking City

Directions Read the selection below. Answer the questions that follow.

Mexico City's Metropolitan Cathedral is sinking! The ground beneath the cathedral is gradually subsiding, or sinking, as well. Subsidence has become a worldwide problem and is most often caused when people pump too much water out of the ground. Depending on the type of soil, large-scale removal of ground water can cause soil and rock to compact, or push together. Eventually the ground settles. Subsidence is generally a slow process but is now considered to be a type of natural disaster, one that occurs in many parts of the world.

Although people have been aware for more than a century that Mexico City is subsiding, the cause of the subsidence only became known in the 1940s. During the mid-1900s, Mexico City officials put measures in place to slow the rate of subsidence. Nevertheless, subsidence continues to be a serious problem. It has resulted in the need to frequently upgrade the city's sewage system. It also has caused damage to the city's roads and a number of historic buildings.

The current use of radar satellite images and GPS monitoring systems shows that Mexico City has subsided at a relatively constant rate over a ten-year period. Highest readings show the city sinking at a rate of 380 mm per year, or approximately 15 inches. Monitoring also shows that the main area of subsidence has shifted east of the downtown area to Lake Texcoco, an area of intense development.

1. What is the major cause of subsidence?

_____

_____

2. Do you think that Mexico City can afford to keep growing? Explain why or why not.

_____

_____

Name _____ Class _____ Date _____

Section Quiz

Directions Answer the following questions using what you learned
in Section 1.

1. _____ In which region of Mexico are
sinkholes most likely to be found?
  a. Mexican Plateau
  b. Baja California
  c. Sonoran Desert
  d. Yucatán Peninsula

2. _____ What effect does altitude have on
Mexico's climate?
  a. As altitude decreases, the temperature
    becomes cooler.
  b. As altitude increases, the temperature
    becomes cooler.
  c. As altitude increases, hurricanes form.
  d. There is very little effect.

3. _____ Which area is a major source of
hydroelectric power?
  a. Baja California
  b. Yucatán Peninsula
  c. Mexican Plateau
  d. Sierra Madre Oriental

4. _____ How does irrigation negatively affect
farmland?
  a. Crops often rot from over-watering.
  b. Irrigation results in salt buildup that
    reduces soil fertility.
  c. The cost of irrigation systems reduces
    profit.
  d. Irrigation washes fertile topsoil away.

5. _____ What type of natural disaster is most
likely to occur in late spring and in early
fall?
  a. tornadoes
  b. floods
  c. earthquakes
  d. hurricanes

6. Complete the table below by describing the impact each
activity has on the environment.

Activity	Environmental Impact
Urban growth	
Clear-cutting	
Overgrazing	

T13

Chapter Atlas

- Model preparing to read by previewing the Key Ideas, Key Terms, headings, visuals, and captions. Have students make predictions about what they will learn. For ELL support, post the prompt, "I predict I will read about . . ."

- Preview and practice reading special-purpose maps by looking at the map of economic activity. Have students identify information the map might contain. Ask, What does the key show? (types of economic activity)

- Preteach this section's high-use Academic Vocabulary and Key Terms using the table on the next page and in-text definitions. Have students practice Key Terms by completing the *Word Wise* page in their journals.

GUIDE ON THE SIDE

Geographic Regions

- **Compare and Contrast** How does Mexico compare with other Latin American nations in terms of size? (Mexico is the third-largest country.)

- **Identify Details** What Mexican peninsula lies west of the Gulf of California? (Baja California)

- **Identify Details** What is Mexico's main landform region? (Mexican Plateau)

Reading Skill

Label an Outline Map While they read, have students identify the Places to Know! on the outline map of the region in the **Student Journal.**

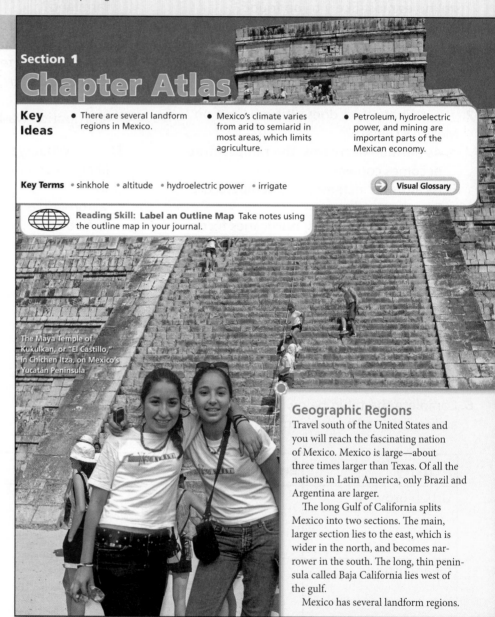

Section 1

Chapter Atlas

Key Ideas
- There are several landform regions in Mexico.
- Mexico's climate varies from arid to semiarid in most areas, which limits agriculture.
- Petroleum, hydroelectric power, and mining are important parts of the Mexican economy.

Key Terms • sinkhole • altitude • hydroelectric power • irrigate

→ **Visual Glossary**

Reading Skill: Label an Outline Map Take notes using the outline map in your journal.

The Maya Temple of Kukulkan, or "El Castillo," in Chichen Itza, on Mexico's Yucatán Peninsula

Geographic Regions

Travel south of the United States and you will reach the fascinating nation of Mexico. Mexico is large—about three times larger than Texas. Of all the nations in Latin America, only Brazil and Argentina are larger.

The long Gulf of California splits Mexico into two sections. The main, larger section lies to the east, which is wider in the north, and becomes narrower in the south. The long, thin peninsula called Baja California lies west of the gulf.

Mexico has several landform regions.

ACADEMIC VOCABULARY

High-Use Word	Definition and Sample Sentence
collapse	*v.* to crumble or fall *The damaged building was about to collapse.*
inadequate	*adj.* not sufficient or suitable *The food was inadequate for so many people.*

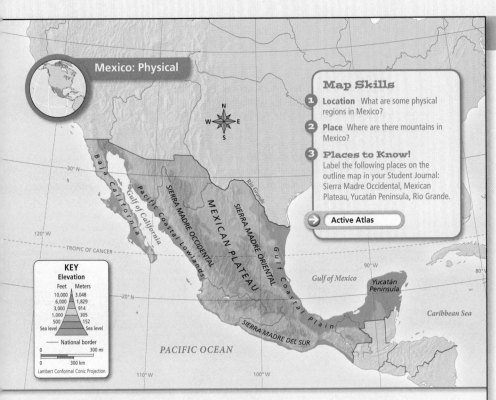

Map Skills

1. **Location** What are some physical regions in Mexico?

2. **Place** Where are there mountains in Mexico?

3. **Places to Know!**
Label the following places on the outline map in your Student Journal: Sierra Madre Occidental, Mexican Plateau, Yucatán Peninsula, Rio Grande.

➜ **Active Atlas**

The main region is the Mexican Plateau, which covers much of the central part of the nation. It has several of Mexico's chief cities, including Mexico City, the capital. The soil in and near Mexico City is soft and settles in places. As a result, some buildings in the city have sunk over the years. Earthquakes can also strike this area and cause great damage.

Flanking the Mexican Plateau are two long mountain chains. Forming the western flank are the Sierra Madre Occidental. East of the plateau rise the Sierra Madre Oriental, which are rich in minerals. These two chains meet at the south of the Mexican Plateau in a region full of volcanoes. The mountains here also have many minerals.

Two lowland regions run alongside the mountains. The narrow Pacific Coastal Lowlands extend from the United States border about halfway down the coast. The wider Gulf Coastal Plain stretches from the border to the Yucatán Peninsula, which juts north into the Gulf of Mexico. The Yucatán is covered by a shell of limestone with many caves underground. Sometimes the roofs of these caves <u>collapse</u>, forming depressions, or sunken areas called **sinkholes**.

collapse, *v.,* to crumble or fall

MAP SKILLS 1. Mexican Plateau, Baja California, Yucatán Peninsula, Pacific and Gulf Central Coastal Plains, Sierra Madres **2.** East and West of the Mexican Plateau **3.** Students should correctly label their maps in the **Student Journal.**

GUIDE ON THE SIDE

- **Identify Details** In what region is Mexico City located? (the Mexican Plateau)

- **Identify Details** What type of natural disaster does the Mexico City area sometimes experience? (earthquakes)

- **Cause and Effect** What causes sinkholes to form in the Yucatán? (The roofs of caves sometimes collapse.)

Map Skills Point out and discuss the physical map.

- Where do Mexico's lowest-lying areas occur? (along the coasts)

- Where are the Sierra Madre mountains located? (in both eastern and western Mexico)

 Active Atlas

Have students visit myworldgeography.com to view more maps of Mexico.

BACKGROUND

A Desert Shared The Sonoran Desert covers approximately 100,000 square miles. It encompasses much of the state of Sonora, Mexico, but also includes Mexico's Baja California peninsula and parts of the southern United States. Its mild winters set the Sonoran Desert apart from other deserts in North America.

The Sonoran experiences two rainy seasons, from July to mid-September and from December to March. Violent thunderstorms are most likely to occur during the summer, while winter rains are more likely to make the desert bloom. The Sonoran Desert supports many forms of life, including some 2,000 plant species.

GUIDE ON THE SIDE

Climate

- **Cause and Effect** How does Mexico's size affect its climate? (Mexico's large size results in climate diversity.)

- **Identify Main Ideas and Details** Where in Mexico are the Sonoran and Chihuahaun deserts? (northern Mexico)

- **Compare and Contrast** How does northern Mexico compare with southern Mexico in terms of precipitation? (Northern Mexico is very dry. Southern Mexico receives much more rain.)

Map Skills Have students use information from the climate map to answer the questions.

- What types of climate occur in northern Mexico? (arid and semiarid)

- Where in Mexico is a humid subtropical region mostly found? (central Mexico)

Active Atlas

Have students visit myworldgeography.com to learn more about Mexico's climate.

Both the Pacific and Gulf lowlands can be hit by hurricanes. The Sierra Madre del Sur cover the south of Mexico. This region includes mountains along the Pacific Coast and rugged valleys.

Mexico's last region is Baja California. This peninsula is about eight times longer than it is wide. Baja California has a rugged coast along the Pacific Ocean, and while the area is mostly arid, there is some potential for agriculture.

Reading Check What is Mexico's main region?

Climate

Mexico has several climate areas. The nation's large size is one reason for climate diversity. Differences in elevation also contribute to different climates.

Baja California and the northern parts of Mexico are very dry. Two large deserts—the Sonoran and Chihuahuan deserts—cover much of northern Mexico.

More than half of Mexico is south of the Tropic of Cancer. Warm, moist air blows off the oceans over these areas. When the air reaches the land, it cools and releases

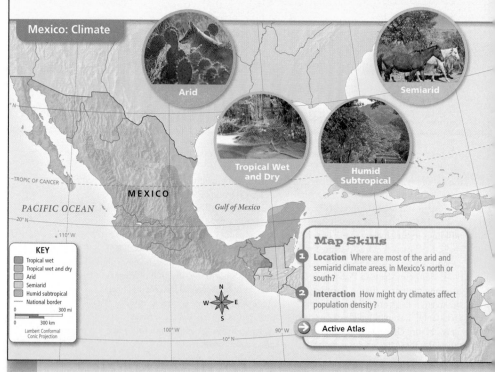

Mexico: Climate

Arid

Semiarid

Tropical Wet and Dry

Humid Subtropical

MEXICO

PACIFIC OCEAN

Gulf of Mexico

TROPIC OF CANCER

KEY
- Tropical wet
- Tropical wet and dry
- Arid
- Semiarid
- Humid subtropical
- National border

0 — 300 mi
0 — 300 km
Lambert Conformal Conic Projection

Map Skills
1. **Location** Where are most of the arid and semiarid climate areas, in Mexico's north or south?
2. **Interaction** How might dry climates affect population density?

Active Atlas

ANSWERS

READING CHECK The Mexican Plateau is Mexico's main region.

MAP SKILLS 1. in Mexico's north **2.** Dry climates might result in low population density.

CORE CONCEPTS: TEMPERATURE

Review Core Concept 3.2 before discussing Mexico's variations in altitude. Review Mexico's location on the planet and how it might affect the country's temperatures. Also review the meaning of *altitude* and how it affects climate. Then have students list ways in which high altitude might affect population distribution and economic activities in Mexico.

water. As a result, the southern part of Mexico receives more rain than the north. People can grow crops in the southern Mexican Plateau. Thick rain forests grow in the Yucatán and southern Mexico.

In the late summer and early fall, hurricanes can hit the tropics. Communities along the coast can be badly damaged by the high winds and heavy rains brought by these powerful storms.

Temperatures in the tropics do not vary much during the year. Farther north, temperature changes are more dramatic.

Climate in Mexico also varies by **altitude,** or height above sea level. The higher you go, the cooler the temperatures are. Even in the tropics, cities on mile-high plateaus have moderate temperatures. If you climb higher, you reach colder land. The tops of mountains are covered with snow.

Mexico's climate patterns have affected where people live. It is very difficult to grow crops in the hot, dry northern areas. As a result, few people live in northern Mexico. The cooler temperatures and heavier rainfall of the southern part of the Mexican Plateau make a better climate for growing food. For this reason, the areas around Mexico City in the south have long been the population centers. The thick rain forests farther south make traveling there difficult. Also, heavy rains wash away the soil, making farming difficult. For these reasons, the rain forest region has relatively few people.

Reading Check What are two reasons that Mexico has many different climate areas?

Closer Look

Ecosystems of Mexico

Mexico's ecosystems host unique animal and plant life. The Sonoran Desert in northwest Mexico is very dry with little vegetation. The Gulf and Pacific coastal lowlands are dry in the north, but support agriculture in the south. Rainforests host dense vegetation and diverse wildlife.

Think Critically How do ecosystems change from north to south?

The pronghorn antelope and the yucca plant are found in the Sonoran Desert. ▶

KEY
- Desert
- Rain forest
- Coastal lowland
- Other

▲ The tarantula is found in the rain forest and lives between 6 and 11 years.

Mexico's gulf coastal lowlands have lagoons and swampy areas.

READING CHECK Mexico's large size and different elevations cause it to have many different climate areas.

THINK CRITICALLY Desert begins in the north. Desert in the east extends into central Mexico. Rainforest is mostly southern, although one area extends north. Coastal lowlands are almost entirely located in the south.

ANSWERS

GOVERNMENT

Dam Causes Controversy Although dams supply much-needed energy, they have become increasingly controversial. In Mexico, so many people objected to the building of La Parota—a dam planned for construction across the Papagayo River near Acapulco—that people sued to stop construction.

Objections to La Parota involved both environmental and human rights issues. Environmental concerns include the flooding of more than 42,000 acres, which would destroy tropical forests and the habitats of endangered species. There also are risks associated with the dam's location in an area of significant seismic activity. Human rights issues revolve around the area's 25,000 inhabitants, many of whom would be displaced by La Parota. In 2009 the Mexican press reported that the government had decided to postpone the dam until after 2018.

Land Resources

- **Cause and Effect** What must Mexico do to develop its untapped oil reserves? (invest in the development of these areas)

- **Identify Main Ideas and Details** What provides about one sixth of Mexico's power? (hydroelectricity)

- **Identify Main Ideas and Details** What is the primary location of Mexico's energy industry? (the Gulf coast)

Map Skills Discuss the map.

- Where is most of Mexico's oil? (in or on the Gulf of Mexico)

- Which natural resources are found in northern Mexico? (natural gas, minerals, corn)

21st Century Learning

Read Special-Purpose Maps Have students develop this skill by using the interactive online tutorial and activities.

Land Resources

The mountains and plateaus of Mexico contain many important resources. Mexico produces more silver than any other nation in the world. Copper and iron are other major metal products. Mexico also mines gold, zinc, and lead.

Mexico's most important natural resource is petroleum. Mexico is one of the top producers of oil in the world. The oil is drilled from wells under the Gulf of Mexico, along the Gulf coast, and in high elevations in the south. The nation has large unused reserves of oil as well. Some of these deposits are difficult to tap, however. Mexico needs to invest more in developing these areas so that it can continue to produce oil.

Mexico also has natural gas in some of the areas that produce oil. Mexico has yet to fully use this resource. About one sixth of the nation's electricity comes from **hydroelectric power,** or power generated by water running through channels in dams. These dams have been built along fast-running rivers on the edges of the central plateau and in high southern elevations.

Much of Mexico's energy industry is along the Gulf coast, where the oil is

myWorld Activity
Mexico's Resources

Mexico: Economic Activity

Map Skills
1. **Region** What region produces most of Mexico's mined resources?
2. **Location** Where are Mexico's oil reserves?

21st Century Learning

Gulf of Mexico

TROPIC OF CANCER

MEXICO

PACIFIC OCEAN

KEY
- Corn
- Oil
- Natural gas
- Mines
- Hydroelectric power
- Industrial area

0   300 mi
0   300 km
Lambert Conformal Conic Projection

MAP SKILLS 1. the northern region
2. on or in the Gulf of Mexico

ECONOMICS

Mexican Oil Cantarell, the reservoir that for years has served as Mexico's primary source of oil, is becoming depleted. Mexico's crude production reached a record high in 2004, at 3.38 million barrels per day (bpd) but fell to 3.26 million bpd in 2006. Predictions indicate that the decline will continue. Although scientists believe that the Gulf of Mexico holds other significant oil reserves, Mexico has been unable to resolve the question of how to finance the technology that oil exploration requires.

The problem is that Pemex, Mexico's oil company, is owned by the state. Although foreign investment is an obvious potential source of capital, the majority of Mexicans are against it. Many fear the loss of jobs.

located. Refineries near Veracruz and in northeastern Mexico turn the oil into various products. In the past, manufacturing plants were clustered in Mexico City. The government has tried to reduce crowding there by encouraging more manufacturing in the north.

Because of mountains, poor soils, and dry climates, only about one fifth of Mexico's land can be used for farming. Less than that is actually farmed. Major crops include corn, wheat, beans, sugar cane, and many fruits and vegetables. Coffee is an important export crop. The waters off the Baja California peninsula support a large fishing industry. Northern Mexico has many cattle ranches.

For several centuries, relatively few people owned large amounts of land in Mexico. The majority of people worked the land for these privileged few. In the 1900s, the government passed laws to break up these large estates and give land to the poor. Now, though, many families have such small holdings that they can only grow enough to feed their families.

Reading Check What is Mexico's most important resource, and where is it found?

A worker turns a valve wheel at a Pemex refinery, Mexico's national oil company. ▼

Oil Production in Mexico

Mexico produces more oil than many countries in the world. While selling oil to other countries has brought money to Mexico, this money has made the country dependent on the amount of oil other countries buy.

2007 Oil Production per Day

United States
8,457,000

Mexico
3,501,000

Iraq*
2,096,500

1 million barrels

*In 2002, the last year before the Iraq War, production was 2,500,000 barrels per day.

SOURCE: *CIA World Factbook*, U.S. Energy Information Administration

Chart Skills
How does Mexico's oil production compare to the United States and Iraq?

21st Century Learning

READING CHECK Oil, Mexico's most important resource, is found along the Gulf coast, under the Gulf of Mexico, and in the Southern Highlands.

CHART SKILLS Mexico's daily production of oil is nearly 5 million barrels less than that of the United States and about 1,400,000 barrels more than Iraq's production.

GOVERNMENT

Border 2012 The United States and Mexico have joined forces to create Border 2012, a program that addresses environmental problems in cities along the U.S.–Mexican border. Some 12 million people live in the border region, with 90 percent living in 14 paired "sister cities." NAFTA has led to rapid growth in these urban areas, as factories have sprung up on the Mexican side to process goods for export to the United States.

Border 2012 addresses six goals, the first three being reduction of water contamination, air pollution, and land contamination. Additional goals are the improvement of environmental health, emergency preparedness and response, and environmental stewardship. To date, progress includes the cleanup of huge numbers of discarded tires, training in the safe use of pesticides, and the development of emergency response procedures.

GUIDE ON THE SIDE

Environmental Impact

- **Cause and Effect** What accounts for Mexico's population growth over the last hundred years? (health improvements)

- **Summarize** What conditions are common in cities along Mexico's northern border? (overcrowding, pollution, lack of proper sanitation)

- **Draw Conclusions** Why is air pollution a major problem in Mexico City? (The city's population uses a huge amount of fossil fuels, which are a major source of air pollution.)

Map Skills Refer students to the population map and circle graph.

- Which large urban areas are located in northern Mexico? (Tijuana, Monterrey)

- What percentage of Mexico's population lives in cities? (76%)

Active Atlas

Have students go to myworldgeography.com to learn more about Mexico's population.

Environmental Impact

Mexico had about six times more people in the early 2000s than it did in the early 1900s. Health improvements were important factors in this population growth. The rate of growth has slowed in recent years, but Mexico's population is still growing faster than that of the United States.

About three quarters of the people now live in cities, far more than in the past. Mexico City is by far the largest city, with nearly one sixth of all Mexicans living in and around the city. In fact, it is one of the largest cities in the world.

Many cities along the border of Mexico and the United States have grown very rapidly in recent years. Many of the new arrivals live in quickly built, <u>inadequate</u> housing. These cities are plagued by overcrowding, and a lack of water and sewer systems.

Pollution from the spread of industry and the growth of these cities has become a major problem in northern Mexico. Air pollution is also a serious problem in

inadequate, *adj.,* not sufficient or suitable

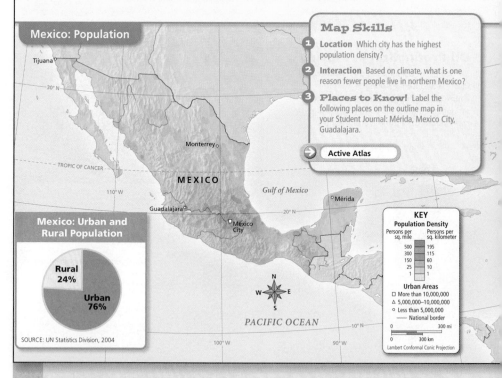

Mexico: Population

Tijuana

30° N

TROPIC OF CANCER

110° W

Monterrey

MEXICO

Gulf of Mexico

Guadalajara

Mérida

20° N

México City

Mexico: Urban and Rural Population

Rural 24%

Urban 76%

SOURCE: UN Statistics Division, 2004

PACIFIC OCEAN

10° N

100° W

90° W

KEY
Population Density

Persons per sq. mile	Persons per sq. kilometer
500	195
300	115
150	60
25	10
1	1

Urban Areas
□ More than 10,000,000
△ 5,000,000–10,000,000
○ Less than 5,000,000
— National border

0   300 mi
0   300 km
Lambert Conformal Conic Projection

Map Skills

1 **Location** Which city has the highest population density?

2 **Interaction** Based on climate, what is one reason fewer people live in northern Mexico?

3 **Places to Know!** Label the following places on the outline map in your Student Journal: Mérida, Mexico City, Guadalajara.

Active Atlas

MAP SKILLS 1. Mexico City
2. Northern Mexico's climate is very dry. **3.** Students should label maps correctly in the **Student Journal.**

SECTION 1 ASSESSMENT 1. Samples: In the Yucatán, cave roofs sometimes collapse, forming sinkholes. Where altitude increases, the air becomes cooler. To produce hydroelectric power, dams are built along fast-running rivers. Farmers'

READING CHECK Northern cities have grown rapidly, resulting in overcrowding, air pollution, and unsanitary conditions.

ANSWERS

ECONOMICS

A Windy Solution The Mexican government has a plan to reduce air pollution by cutting carbon emissions in half. In response to that goal, two of Mexico's largest energy companies are building a huge wind farm. The facility is expected to reduce one company's CO_2 emissions by 600,000 metric tons annually.

The wind farm is located in the state of Oaxaca on the narrow land bridge separating the Pacific Ocean and the Gulf of Mexico. Typical wind speeds there range from 15 to 22 miles per hour, which is nearly ideal for wind turbines. When completed, the farm will be the world's largest, with 167 wind turbines.

Mexico City, where clouds of unhealthy air can hang above the city for days.

The growth of Mexico's population has led to increased demand on the land. Farmers need to **irrigate,** or bring water to the land, in drier areas. Over time, though, salt builds up in the soil of irrigated fields. That salt ruins the fertility of the soil. Overgrazing by cattle is another concern. Because of irrigation and overgrazing, some of Mexico's fragile land is becoming desert.

Another environmental issue is deforestation in the south, where poor farmers cut down and burn trees to open new land for farming. Because the heavy rains there wash nutrients out of the soil, the land can produce crops for only a few years. Farmers then move on, cutting down trees in a new area. Some of the southern forests have valuable woods. Harvesting of these trees also contributes to the rapid destruction of Mexico's forests.

Reading Check How has rapid population growth affected northern Mexico?

Mexico City is located in a valley, and it is difficult for polluted air to escape the city. Population contributes to the amount of pollution, which leads to sickness.

19.4 million people
4 million cars
20 million lost workdays annually

Source: UN Data; SMA; Third World Cities

Section 1 Assessment

Key Terms

1. Use the following terms to describe Mexico: sinkhole, altitude, hydroelectric power, irrigate.

Key Ideas

2. What natural disasters can strike Mexico?

3. What are Mexico's mineral resources?

4. How has Mexico's population changed in recent decades?

Think Critically

5. **Identify Evidence** Why does northern Mexico have relatively few people?

6. **Synthesize** How do environmental challenges in northern and southern Mexico differ?

? Essential Question

How much does geography shape a country?

7. What is one reason much of Mexico's population growth has occurred in and around Mexico City? Go to your Student Journal to record your answer.

GUIDE ON THE SIDE

Cause and Effect Have students read to determine how human activity affects the environment.

- What is causing some of Mexico's land to turn into desert? (overgrazing and irrigation)

- Why are forests being cleared? (to create land for farming; to harvest valuable wood)

- What is one effect of deforestation? (soil degradation)

Analyze Visuals Use the image to explore causes and effects of air pollution.

- Why are the mountains in the background barely visible? (The air is polluted.)

- Why is there so much smog? (Millions of cars create considerable air pollution.)

need to irrigate has reduced soil fertility. **2.** hurricanes, volcanic eruptions **3.** oil, petroleum, copper, iron, gold, zinc, and lead **4.** Population is still increasing but at a slower rate. **5.** Few people live in the north because it is difficult to grow crops there. **6.** in the north, air pollution and lack of water; in the south, deforestation and desertification **7.** Manufacturing plants are clustered around Mexico City.

ANSWERS

Rise and Fall of the Aztecs

OBJECTIVES

Students will

- identify Aztec accomplishments and reasons for their decline.
- **21st Century Learning** describe effects of Aztec culture on Mexican culture.
- **ELL** use English to differentiate between peninsulares, criollos, and mestizos.

SET EXPECTATIONS

In this case study, students will

- read Rise and Fall of the Aztecs.
- design museum exhibits about the lasting influence of Aztec culture.

1 Connect

Review with students what they already know about how the arrival of Cortes in Mexico affected Native Americans. Have students predict how the Spanish defeated the Aztecs.

> **ELL** **Intermediate** Model this sentence for students to use: *I predict that the Spanish*

used _____ to defeat the Aztecs. Provide a word bank of possible nouns, such as *horses*, *allies*, *skill*, and *cannons*. Then explain that all of the choices are correct.

2 Learn

Preview Have students preview pictures and headings. Ask them if they think the following statement is true or false: "Past civilizations have helped to shape Mexican culture today." Have students make predictions in three categories—language, food, and artifacts.

Read While students read Rise and Fall of the Aztecs, ask questions found in the **Guide on the Side** to build understanding of Key Ideas and objectives. Encourage students to think about the contradiction of a civilization that is defeated but whose culture continues on.

> **ELL** **Early Advanced** Draw a pyramid on the board to show the levels of colonial society. Point to each, indicating lowest, middle, and highest. Then model this sentence for students to use: _____ made up the _____ level of society.

L2 Extra Support While students read, have them take notes in a two-column table with the headings *Aztec Technological Achievements* and *Spanish Technological Achievements*.

myWorld Activity: Mini-Museum
Assign students to work in small groups to design a display for an exhibit on the influence of Aztec culture on Mexico today. Assign groups one of the following categories of influence: food, language, artifacts. Have students use *Activity Support: Exhibit Design* to plan their display. Then allow time for students to make and exhibit their display as a model, Web page, poster, or form of their choosing. Have students view each other's posted displays. **(Visual)**

30 min

3 Understand

Review Have students work in pairs to read and identify the main ideas and details of each heading in the Case Study. Then review those ideas as a class. Debate which idea is more important—the fact of the Aztecs' decline or the fact of their lasting cultural influence.

Assess Check students' answers to the Assessment questions for completeness and accuracy. Return to the statement you discussed

earlier: "Past civilizations have helped to shape Mexican culture today." Discuss how information in the text supports or negates the statement.

Remediate Post a concept diagram on the board and label the center oval *Aztec to Mexican*. Have students use each visual in the Case Study to come up with one detail to fill in the surrounding ovals with examples of Aztec culture that have influenced Mexican culture.

Name _____ Class _____ Date _____

myWorld Activity Support   **Exhibit Design**

Mini-Museum

Directions Work with your group to design and make a display about your assigned aspect of Aztec culture and its influence on Mexico today. Turn your classroom into a miniature museum. The title of the exhibit could be Lasting Influences. Visit each other's displays to learn about how the Aztecs made a lasting impact on Mexican culture. Your displays could be Web pages, posters, or 3-dimensional models. Consider adding sound recordings to your exhibit.

Category of Aztec Influence (Check one.)   ☐ Food

☐ Artifacts

☐ Language

Examples of Aztec Influence on _____ **in Mexico Today**

1. _____

_____

2. _____

_____

3. _____

_____

Type of Display (Check one.)   ☐ Poster   ☐ 3-dimensional Model   ☐ Web site

☐ Other _____

Exhibit Plan Draw and/or describe with words what your museum exhibit would look like and what information it would contain. Then make your display and share it with the class.

QUICK FACTS

The Aztec Empire Share these facts about the Empire at its most powerful.

- Population: 5 to 6 million
- Size: 80,000 square miles
- Center of Power: Tenochtitlán

Tenochtitlán covered about 5 square miles and had a population of about 140,000. It formed alliances with two neighboring states, Texcoco and Tlacopan. This was known as the Triple Alliance.

Becoming Powerful

- **Identify Details** Where did the Aztecs settle? (in the Valley of Mexico)

- **Summarize** What farming methods did the Aztecs use? (terracing and irrigation)

- **Cause and Effect** How did the Aztecs make more land for farming? (by building fields within a lake)

Case Study

Rise and Fall of the Aztecs

Key Ideas
- The Aztecs rose to power by conquering smaller groups of native people and learning from the cultures of those smaller groups.
- Although the Spanish took over the Aztec empire, much of Aztec culture remains in Mexico today, including the Nahuatl language.

Key Terms • peninsular • criollo • mestizo • Nahuatl

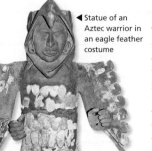
◀ Statue of an Aztec warrior in an eagle feather costume

In what is today Mexico, the Aztecs built a large Native American empire. Although they did not control the region for as long as the Olmec or Maya peoples, their population grew quickly. Soon they controlled many native groups in the area, and their capital, Tenochtitlán, became a center of culture and trade in the region. The Aztec empire was so large that its culture spread widely. As a result, the Aztecs left lasting effects on Mexico.

Becoming Powerful

The Aztecs settled in the Valley of Mexico—where Mexico City now is—in 1325. Aztec tradition says that a people named the Toltecs dominated central Mexico at the time. Researchers are not sure that the Toltecs ever existed. Clearly, though, the Aztecs built on the foundations of earlier peoples—and expanded those traditions.

Following earlier practices, they built terraces on the steep valley walls. These step-like patches of land held water, allowing farmers to grow crops on hillsides. The Aztecs also built irrigation ditches to bring water to their fields. The most impressive Aztec achievement, though, was the way they grew crops within Lake Texcoco. The Aztecs built islands by layering mud on top of woven branches. Then they used these islands to grow crops to feed a growing population.

The Aztecs were not powerful at first. Over time, though, military leaders led the Aztecs to conquer other peoples. Their rule could be harsh, as they turned some of the conquered peoples into slaves. They killed some of those slaves as sacrifices to their gods, believing that doing so would ensure the gods' protection.

Reading Check How did the Aztecs turn a lake into fields for farming?

READING CHECK The Aztecs wove reeds and branches together to form islands on which to farm.

GEOGRAPHY

The Venice of the New World Located south of downtown Mexico City, Xochimilco is a unique vestige of Aztec civilization. Its name in Nahuatl, the Aztec language, means "where the flowers grow," and it is all that remains of the artificial islands built by the Aztecs. These islands, or chinampas, once covered an estimated area of 400 square kilometers. Today, due to urban sprawl, the area has shrunk to about 25 square kilometers.

In 1987 UNESCO chose Xochimilco as a World Heritage Site. However, Xochimilco may be in danger of disappearing altogether if developers continue to fill in the canals in order to build on them. Encompassing streets as well as canals and chinampas, Xochimilco is home to more than 300,000 people. Water in the canals is polluted and access to city services is limited. Yet on the chinampas, flowers and vegetables continue to grow in great profusion.

The Spanish Arrive

When Hernán Cortés landed in Mexico, he had only 500 soldiers with him. The soldiers faced an empire with an army of thousands. Nevertheless, Cortés and his soldiers defeated the Aztec empire.

Several factors contributed to the Spaniards' success. The Spanish were armed with muskets and cannons, which were far more powerful than the clubs and blades used by Aztecs. The Spanish also had horses that allowed the army to move quickly. The Aztecs had no horses.

The Spanish also benefited because many native peoples who had been conquered by the Aztecs joined the Spanish to fight the Aztecs. These peoples had long resented harsh Aztec rule.

Finally, the Spanish unknowingly brought European diseases to Mexico. Native Americans had never been exposed to illnesses like measles and smallpox. Without defenses against these diseases, hundreds of thousands of native people died.

Reading Check Why did other native peoples join the Spanish in fighting the Aztecs?

A City on a Lake

Mexico City was built on top of the Aztec capital of Tenochtitlán. The Aztecs built the city on an island in the middle of Lake Texcoco. Aztec construction efforts slowly filled in the lake. Over the years, some modern buildings built on this water-logged soil have begun to sink into the ground.

The Plaza de las Tres Culturas, or "Plaza of the Three Cultures," is a mix of Aztec, Spanish colonial, and modern buildings. ▼

The map below shows modern Mexico City with the outline of the former Lake Texcoco. ▼

Ecatepec de Morelos

Plaza of Three Cultures

MÉXICO CITY   Nezahualcóyotl

KEY
- ○ City today
- ═ Major roads today
- ── Minor roads today
- ▢ Lake Texcoco, 1521
- △ Plaza of Three Cultures

READING CHECK Some native peoples joined the Spanish because they resented Aztec rule.

The Spanish Arrive

- **Cause and Effect** How did superior technology help Cortés defeat the Aztecs? (The Spanish had guns and cannons, which were superior to the clubs and blades of the Aztecs.)

- **Draw Conclusions** How did disease affect the outcome of Cortés's invasion? (The spread of European diseases weakened the ability of the Aztecs to resist the Spanish.)

Analyze Visuals Challenge students to identify evidence of the following three cultures in the image on this page.

- Aztec (steps of a pyramid)
- colonial (the cathedral)
- modern (the building at left)

CORE CONCEPTS: FAMILIES AND SOCIETIES

Review Core Concept 7.2 before discussing the nature of society in Mexico under Spanish colonial rule. Review the characteristics of various societies. Ask students to identify or describe the type of society that existed under Spanish rule (layered, stratified, and hierarchical). You may wish to have them draw and label a pyramid to illustrate the society. Point out that as the pyramid gets taller, the size of the social class becomes smaller. Ask whether they think this system was fair, and why or why not. Ask how the system may have affected present-day society in Mexico.

GUIDE ON THE SIDE

Effect of Spanish Rule

- **Identify Main Ideas** What did the Spanish conquerors gain? (vast estates)

- **Summarize** How did the Spanish treat the Native Americans? (The Spanish forced the Native Americans to farm and work in the mines. They allowed them few rights.)

- **Identify Details** Who were the peninsulares? What position did they hold in colonial society? (The peninsulares came to Mexico from Spain. They held the top position.)

Analyze Visuals

- **Draw Conclusions** Do you think the chinampas were well-built? Explain. (yes, because some still exist today)

Garden on a Lake

Chinampas allowed the Aztecs to grow enough food to feed their ever-expanding population. In the shallow parts of Lake Texcoco, builders drove posts into the bottom of the lake. Between these posts, layers of woven branches and mud created a base to grow crops. Willow trees were planted so the roots would anchor the beds to the lake below.

It took about eight days of digging mud and weaving strips of wood to build a chinampa. ▼

Original canals and chinampas still exist today.

Effect of Spanish Rule

Spanish rule changed society in Mexico. When the Spanish took control of Tenochtitlán, they built new buildings and renamed it Mexico City. Cortés and his soldiers were given vast estates, where they forced Native Americans to farm. Native peoples were also put to work in gold and silver mines. Spanish landowners often treated them harshly. They had few rights.

The Roman Catholic Church played an important role in changing Mexico. Missionaries converted native people to Christianity, which helped establish Spanish customs.

Colonial Mexico developed a new social order. At the top of society were the **peninsulares,** people who came to Mexico from Spain. Although they made up the smallest number of the population, the peninsulares held the most important government jobs. Next highest were the **criollos,** people of Spanish descent who were born in Mexico. Criollos were prohibited from having the highest government posts. Criollos eventually resented the fact that their opportunities were limited by the peninsulares. The next class of people were **mestizos,** or people with mixed Spanish and native backgrounds. Some mestizos paid the government so they could be called criollos. At the bottom of the social ladder were native peoples. The greatest number of people in colonial society were native.

Reading Check **What position did native peoples hold in Spanish colonial society?**

READING CHECK Native peoples held the lowest position.

READING CHECK The Spanish built Mexico City on top of Tenoctitlán.

HISTORY

Written Records After defeating the Aztecs, the Spanish destroyed many Aztec codices, or books. The destruction of this ancient source material has made it especially challenging for historians to interpret the Aztec civilization. However, some books remain, including a codex from the 1500s that contains a detailed drawing of an Aztec temple.

The drawing shows a stepped pyramid with side-by-side stairways. Each stairway leads to a temple at the pyramid's top. The roof of each temple is decorated with symbols connected to an Aztec god. The temple honoring the rain god Tlaloc has broad bands of blue that symbolize rain. The temple honoring the war god Huitzilopochtli is decorated with human skulls. The drawing illustrates the importance of artifacts as keys to the understanding of past civilizations.

Reminders

The Aztec heritage lives on in many ways in modern Mexico. When the government built a giant outdoor stadium in the 1960s, it proudly named the new structure after the Native American empire. Aztec Stadium still stands in Mexico City after hosting the 1968 Summer Olympic Games and countless other events.

The **Nahuatl** language of the Aztecs lives on in Mexico today. Many words for foods common to Mexico were absorbed into Spanish from Nahuatl. Examples are *avocado, chili, chocolate,* and *tomato.* Such animal names as coyote and ocelot are also Nahuatl words.

Some remains of Aztec life can be seen in Mexico's landscape. The huge open plaza called the Zócalo in the center of Mexico City was the site of a giant plaza in Aztec times. Still, since the Spanish built Mexico City on top of Tenochtitlán, Aztec remains are hidden. Getting at these buildings might mean damaging important buildings from Spanish colonial times.

Sometimes, though, researchers uncover new information that can change the way we look at the past. Recently, an Aztec pyramid was discovered in Mexico

▲ A modern market where chilis, avocados, and tomatoes are sold.

▲ The Mexican flag shows an image from an Aztec myth. The myth told the Aztecs to settle where they saw an eagle on a cactus eating a snake. The Aztecs saw this eagle on an island in Lake Texcoco.

City. Scientists think the structure might be as much as 800 years old. If it is in fact that old, this discovery may prove that the Aztecs settled in the Valley of Mexico earlier than historians had thought.

Reading Check Why are Aztec buildings in Mexico City hidden?

Reminders

- **Compare and Contrast** How are Aztec Stadium and the Zócalo different? How are they similar? (The stadium is modern, while the Zócalo dates back to the Aztecs. Both are large open spaces in Mexico City and both are reminders of the Aztecs.)

- **Identify Details** What Aztec legacy is part of daily life throughout Mexico? (words from Nahuatl, the language of the Aztecs)

Analyze Visuals Have students compare the images.

- Which aspects of culture does each image illustrate? (market: food and language; flag: myth)

Assessment

1. Why did the Aztecs sacrifice some of the people they conquered to their gods?

2. What factors helped the Spanish conquer the Aztec Empire?

3. What was the difference between peninsulares and criollos?

4. How have parts of Aztec culture continued in Mexico today?

5. What are the similarities between the Aztecs and Spanish in how each group treated the people they conquered?

ASSESSMENT 1. The Aztecs believed that human sacrifice would ensure that the gods would protect them. **2.** superior weapons, horses, and the support of native peoples **3.** Peninsulares came to Mexico from Spain. Criollos were of Spanish descent but born in Mexico. **4.** through Nahuatl words that have been absorbed by Spanish, through Aztec artifacts such as the Zócalo, and through myth **5.** Like the Spanish, the Aztecs enslaved some of the people they conquered.

History of Mexico

OBJECTIVES

Students will know

- the characteristics and accomplishments of Mexico's indigenous people.
- the factors that led to political independence.

Students will be able to

- analyze causes and effects of Mexico's historic events.
- decide whether or not to excavate artifacts.

SET EXPECTATIONS

In this section, students will

- read History of Mexico.
- choose sides about uncovering Tenochtitlán.
- go On Assignment in Mexico and explore the history of Carolina's people.

CORE CONCEPTS

You may wish to teach or reteach the following lessons from the Core Concepts Handbook:

- What Is Culture?, pp. 86–87
- Cultural Diffusion and Change, pp. 96–97
- Foundations of Government, pp. 104–105

KEY

Differentiated Instruction		English Language Instruction		
L1 Special Needs	**L2** Extra Support	**ELL** Beginner	**ELL** Early Intermediate	**ELL** Intermediate
L3 On-Level	**L4** Challenge	**ELL** Early Advanced	**ELL** Advanced	

1 Connect
Make learning meaningful

Make Connections Ask students how the past has helped to shape the community where they live. Provide prompts such as origin of settlers, traditional foods, religions, style of buildings, and local traditions.

ELL Advanced Ask students to give examples of historic events that shaped their family's home countries.

Activate Prior Knowledge Remind students that in earlier chapters they read about European settlement in North America and how it affected Native Americans. Ask them to predict the effect of Spanish settlements in Mexico.

L2 Extra Support Draw students' attention to how the visuals in the United States and Canada chapter reflect the effects of European settlements on Native Americans. Have students use these pictures to make parallel predictions.

Prepare Follow the steps in the section **Preview.** Preteach the Key Terms. Then have students complete *Word Wise* in their journal using in-text clues and the glossary for help.

2 Experience
Teach knowledge and skills

Read Use **Background** notes and **Guide on the Side** questions to model active reading. Have students use *Take Notes* in their **Student Journal** to analyze causes and effects of events in Mexico's history. Have students complete **21st Century Online Tutor** *Analyze Cause and Effect* and apply what they learn to reading the section.

L4 Challenge Break the word *enlightenment* into parts and help students to make predictions about word meaning. Discuss related words such as *enlightened*.

ELL Intermediate Illustrate the unfair land distribution by using chalk to mark out three even areas on the floor. Give two students sticky-note name tags that say Wealthy Landowner, and several students tags saying Poor Farmers, translating the tags as necessary. Have each Landowner stand in one of the sections, while the remaining students share the third. Ask whether the division is fair.

 Practice: myWorld Activity Students will make a decision about archaeological excavation in Mexico City and then debate their position. **Step-by-Step Instructions** and **More Activities** follow on p. T18.

SECTION 2 RESOURCE GUIDE

FOR THE STUDENT

my worldgeography.com   Student Center

- Timeline

Student Edition (print and online)

- History of Mexico

Student Journal (print and online)

- Section 2 Word Wise
- Section 2 Take Notes

21st Century Learning Online Tutor

- Analyze Cause and Effect
- Make Decisions

FOR THE TEACHER

my worldgeography.com   Teacher Center

- Online Lesson Planner
- Presentations for Projection
- SuccessTracker

ProGuide: Middle America

- Lesson Plan, p. T16
- myWorld Activity Step-by-Step Instructions, p. T18
- Activity Support: Cost-benefit Analysis, p. T19
- myWorld Geography Enrichment, p. T20
- Section Quiz, p. T21

Accelerating the Progress of ELLs

- Peer Learning Strategies, p. 46

3 Understand
Assess understanding

Review Review *Word Wise* and *Take Notes* in the Student Journal.

Assess Knowledge and Skills Use the Section Assessment and Section Quiz to check students' progress.

Assess Understanding Review students' responses to the Section Assessment Essential Question prompt.

Remediate Use these strategies to review and remediate.

If students struggle to . . .	Try these strategies.
Follow the chronology of Mexico's historic events	Help the class make a giant timeline. Clarify students' understanding of centuries, years, and the order of months.
Describe the Mexican Revolution	Post a cause-and-effect graphic organizer with some events filled in already for students to complete.
Comprehend *aqueduct*	Use straws and toothpicks to build aqueduct models.

ELL Support

ELL Objective Students will use English to express a sequence of events.

Cultural Connections To connect students to Mexico's early civilizations, ask them to think about the early history of their home countries. Have them draw something representative of that history, such as a person, an event, or an artifact. Then help them describe their drawing.

ELL Early Intermediate Content Tip Write the numbers 1, 2, and 3 on the board. Under each, write appropriate modifiers such as *first, second,* and *third* that may be used to describe a sequence. Perform a series of actions and indicate which word applies to each action.

ELL Activity Have partners read the section on early Mexico. Have them write the name of each early culture on a different index card. Then they should place the index cards in the correct order and say aloud three sequence sentences showing the order of the three civilizations. **(Verbal/Kinesthetic)**

myWorld Activity   **Step-by-Step Instructions**

 30 min

To Dig or Not To Dig

OBJECTIVES

Students will

- determine the potential costs and benefits of destroying a shopping mall in order to conduct an archaeological dig at Tenochtitlán.
- debate whether to conduct the dig.

LEARNING STYLE

- Verbal
- Logical

21st Century Learning

- Make Decisions

MATERIALS

- Activity Support: Cost-benefit Analysis, p. T19

Activity Steps

1. Remind the students that the ruins of Tenochtitlán exist underneath Mexico City. Tell them they are going to examine the costs and benefits of conducting an archaeological dig to uncover the ruins of the historic city.

   L2 Extra Support Post a concept web and complete it with students in order to review the significance of Tenochtitlán.

   ELL Early Intermediate/Intermediate Explain the meaning of the word *archaeologist:* a scientist who studies remains of the past. Point out appropriate visuals and/or show students images of archaeologists at work and archaeological finds.

2. Have students complete *Activity Support: Cost-benefit Analysis* to itemize the costs and benefits of the archaeological dig and prepare to debate their views.

3. Students should then debate whether the costs of demolishing a shopping center outweigh the value of the Tenochtitlán dig and of potentially recovering the treasures of the lost city. Students may debate a partner or work in pairs to debate another pair. Assign moderators for each debate. Invite volunteers to model making and responding to arguments.

   L4 Challenge Have students use images found online to make a display of an archaeological dig of Aztec ruins.

4. After the debates are completed, take a class vote for or against the dig.

More Activities From myWorld Teachers

 Local Connections Post the following quote: "I came to escape persecution." Have students first journal and then discuss how this immigrant's reason for coming to the United States compares with reasons that draw immigrants from Mexico to the United States today. **(Interpersonal/Verbal)**

Compare Civilizations To help students differentiate between Mexico's ancient

civilizations, post three concept webs on the board labeled Olmec, Maya, and Aztec. Fill in the webs as a class and discuss similarities and differences. **(Logical)**

Ancient Rap Have students write a rap telling the history of the Olmecs, Maya, and Aztecs. Raps should tell a story and have refrains that rhyme. **(Rhythmic/Verbal)**

 **my worldgeography.com** **Teacher Center**   Find additional resources in the online Teacher Center.

Name _____ Class _____ Date _____

myWorld Activity Support **Cost-benefit Analysis**

To Dig or Not to Dig

Directions Imagine that Archaeology University has presented
a proposal to conduct a dig to access ruins of Tenochtitlán, which
lies beneath Mexico City. However, a shopping mall must first be
demolished. List the costs and benefits of this proposal. Then take
a position for or against conducting the dig.

Proposed Archaeological Dig to Access the Ruins of Tenochtitlán

Costs of Destroying the Shopping Mall	Benefits of Digging up Tenochtitlán

Get Ready to Debate! Prepare to debate the dig with fellow
classmates.

Take a Position ___ For the dig   ___ Against the dig

My Argument The facts that support my position outweigh
the facts against it because . . .

_____

_____

_____

Class Vote ___ For   ___ Against

T19

Name _____ Class _____ Date _____

Enrichment: Maize Makes History

Directions Read the selection below. Answer the questions that follow.

Thousands of years ago the first farmer in Mexico planted a seed. The seed was an offshoot of maize, or corn. Its planting marked the beginning of agriculture in the Americas. Scientists believe that maize was first cultivated in southwest Mexico about 8,700 years ago. Its cultivation quickly spread to southeast Mexico and to Central and South America.

Agriculture made it possible for people to settle in one place because they did not have to search for food. Settlement led eventually to the development of the Olmec civilization. The Olmecs placed great value on corn, not only as a source of food but as a symbol of birth, growth, and life after death. They sometimes incorporated symbols of the plant into ceremonial objects, such as masks.

Paleobotanists, the scientists who study the history of plants, have recently made a number of discoveries about the early cultivation of maize. Scientists now believe that early farmers probably cultivated maize from teosinte, a wild ancestor of corn. As scientific tools become more advanced, scientists are able to study the remains of ancient plants in greater detail. Recent studies have focused on phytoliths. Phytoliths are microscopic, or very small, mineral deposits that occur in a plant's leaves, stems, and roots. By examining the shape of a phytolith, scientists can tell whether it belonged to a maize plant or a corn plant. The presence of corn phytoliths indicates that people practiced agriculture in a particular area.

1. Why was corn so important to the development of early civilizations in Mexico?

_____

_____

2. How does the study of ancient plant remains help in our understanding of history?

_____

_____

Name _____ Class _____ Date _____

Section Quiz

Directions Answer the following questions using what you learned in Section 2.

1. _____ What marked the beginning of agriculture in the Americas?
   a. Native peoples began raising goats.
   b. The hoe was invented.
   c. Native peoples began growing maize.
   d. The Spanish arrived.

2. _____ Why did the Aztecs build aqueducts?
   a. to prevent flooding
   b. to collect rain water
   c. to improve sewage systems
   d. to carry water to their capital

3. _____ How did the Maya use astronomy?
   a. to predict horoscopes
   b. to develop accurate calendars
   c. to explain past events
   d. to choose names for their children

4. _____ The Olmec influenced later Native Americans through
   a. trade.
   b. religion.
   c. language.
   d. art.

5. _____ Which of the following was largely responsible for the Mexican Revolution?
   a. separation from Spain
   b. the overthrow of Maximilian
   c. widespread poverty
   d. a lack of women's rights

6. Fill in the timeline with the letters of the events shown in the box.

A. Mexico revolts against Spain.	B. Mexico wins independence from Spain.	C. Mexico declares a new constitution.	D. Beginning of the Mexican Revolution	E. Cortés arrives.

1519   1810   1821   1910   1917

History of Mexico

- Model preparing to read by previewing the Key Ideas, Key Terms, headings, visuals, and captions. Have students make predictions about what they will learn. For ELL support, post the prompt, "I predict I will read about . . ."

- Preview and practice analyzing cause and effect with examples from your community's history.

- Teach this section's high-use Academic Vocabulary using the table on the next page. Have students practice Academic Vocabulary and Key Terms by completing the *Word Wise* page in their journal.

Early Mexico

- **Identify Main Ideas** What marked the beginning of agriculture in the Americas? (the growing of maize)

- **Compare and Contrast** How does the writing system of the Olmec differ from our own? (They used symbols instead of letters.)

- **Draw Conclusions** What indicates that the Olmec civilization was advanced? (It had a political system and a religion. The Olmec developed a calendar and a writing system.)

 Reading Skill

Analyze Cause and Effect
While they read, have students practice this skill by completing the *Take Notes* graphic organizer in the **Student Journal.**

Section 2

History of Mexico

Key Ideas
- Mexico's original people—the Olmecs, Maya, and Aztecs—settled in the area surrounding and including today's Mexico City.
- Enlightenment ideas played a part in Mexico's independence from Spain, similar to the United States in its fight for independence.
- Mexico has sometimes struggled to provide opportunities for all of its citizens, despite economic growth.

Key Terms • maize • astronomy • aqueduct • conquistador • Mexican Revolution   Visual Glossary

 Reading Skill: Analyze Cause and Effect Take notes using the graphic organizer in your journal.

Pendant depicting a Maya ruler, from A.D. 600–1521 ▼

E arly civilizations in Mexico were able to take great advantage of the resources available to them. These societies developed complex farming techniques. Through studying the stars and planets, they were able to develop very accurate calendars. Spanish conquerors arrived in the 1500s, bringing disease that killed many native people. Many native Mexicans were forced into slavery and poverty. The struggles of these early years continued into the 1900s.

Early Mexico
The first people to live in what is now Mexico settled in the area thousands of years ago. They survived by hunting animals and gathering plants. About 7,000 years ago, native peoples first began growing a wild grass called **maize,** or corn. This step marked the beginning of agriculture in the Americas.

Over time, native peoples added other crops, including beans, squash, and chili peppers. As they produced more food, their population grew and they formed larger communities.

Olmec Rule Around 1500 B.C., the Olmec civilization arose along Mexico's Gulf coast, near Tabasco and Veracruz. The Olmecs developed a complex political system, a religion, and a system of writing. Olmec writing used hieroglyphics, in which symbols stand for words. The Olmecs also developed a calendar.

The Olmecs traded with nearby peoples. Through this trade, the Olmecs influenced Native American cultures that came later.

ACADEMIC VOCABULARY

High-Use Word	Definition and Sample Sentence
convert	*v.* to cause someone to adopt a different religion *Priests tried to convert the native peoples to Catholicism.*
estate	*n.* a large piece of land or property *She lived on the largest estate in Italy.*

Maya Civilization The Maya followed the Olmecs as the leading native culture in the region. The Maya lived in what are now southern Mexico, Guatemala, and Belize. They built several dozen cities with thousands of people. These cities had pyramid-shaped temples of stone decorated with sculptures. The Maya also recorded the histories of their rulers.

The Maya excelled at **astronomy,** the study of the stars and planets. They used their learning to construct several calendar systems that worked together to guide their farmers and to plan religious ceremonies.

Maya civilization declined around A.D. 900. Still, Maya cities continued in the Yucatán Peninsula. Thousands of Maya still live in Mexico today.

Emergence of the Aztecs In the 1400s, a new power, the Aztecs, arose in Mexico.

The Aztecs settled in the Valley of Mexico—where Mexico City now is—in the 1300s. They built their capital, Tenochtitlán, on an island in the middle of a lake. With 150,000 people, the city was the largest ever built by Native Americans.

The Aztecs were skilled farmers who grew corn, squash, beans, and other foods. The Aztec were also excellent engineers. They built **aqueducts,** or channels that carried water, to their capital, and canals to make transportation easier.

The Aztecs also had a strong army. After A.D. 1500, they had conquered and controlled 5 million people or more.

Reading Check **What was remarkable about Tenochtitlán?**

Ancient Civilizations of Mexico

Ancient Mexico was home to some of the most complex civilizations in the Western Hemisphere. The Olmecs, Maya, and Aztecs existed at different times in Mexico's history, although each had effects long after the decline of their civilizations.

Timeline

▲ **Olmecs B.C. 1500** Olmec art influenced later cultures in ancient Mexico.

Maya A.D. 300–900 Maya weaving techniques still survive today. ▶

▲ **Aztecs A.D. 1200–1521** Montezuma II ruled over the Aztec empire, which influences Mexican culture today.

Identify Main Ideas Discuss characteristics of Maya and Aztec civilizations.

- What was the basis of the Maya calendar system? (astronomy)
- What structures are typical of Maya cities? (pyramid-shaped temples)
- Where did the Aztecs build their capital city? (where Mexico City is now)

Analyze Visuals Have students compare and contrast the images.

- How are the three images similar? (All show an aspect of culture.)
- In what ways are they different? (Sample: The Maya and Aztec images show activities. The Olmec image does not.)

 Timeline

Have students go to myworldgeography.com to learn more about the Olmecs, Maya, and Aztecs.

READING CHECK Tenochtitlán was built on an island in the middle of a lake.

HISTORY

Roman Catholic Influence The arrival of the Spanish in the New World was not limited to conquistadors. Accompanying the soldier-explorers were Catholic priests, who set about converting the native peoples.

Among the early arrivals was Juan de Zumárraga, who traveled to Mexico in 1528. A Franciscan, he became the colony's first bishop and the official protector of Mexico's native people.

De Zumárraga was committed to converting the indigenous population and to introducing them to Spanish civilization. He worked to improve conditions in New Spain and helped found Santa Cruz de Tlatelolco, a college for native Americans. De Zumárraga also helped bring the New World's first printing press to Mexico, which printed religious manuals he had written. Unfortunately, de Zumárraga also destroyed native manuscripts.

GUIDE ON THE SIDE

Struggle for Power

- **Sequence** How does the mural document Azec history? (by showing the great Aztec capital, its conquest by the Spanish, and resulting Spanish influence)

- **Identify Details** How does the first image express the greatness of the empire? (It shows a huge city and many active people.)

Spanish Rule to Independence

- **Draw Conclusions** Why did the Spanish seek out the Aztecs? (They hoped to gain silver and gold.)

- **Cause and Effect** What effect did the arrival of Cortés have on the Aztec Empire? (His arrival led to the destruction of the empire.)

- **Infer** Why might Cortés have chosen to build Mexico City on the former site of Tenochtitlán? (to show Spain's superiority)

myWorld Activity

To Dig or Not to Dig Find Step-by-Step Instructions and an Activity Support on pp. T18–T19.

Struggle for POWER

Diego Rivera became a well-known artist from Mexico in the early 1900s. His art outlining Mexico's history appears in the National Palace in Mexico City. The paintings begin with the Aztecs, whose empire was reaching its height of power when the Spanish arrived. Seeking gold, the Spanish soon overpowered the Aztecs.

▲ Tenochtitlán, the Aztec capital, was one of the largest cities in the world, with advanced engineering and a complex economy.

convert, *v.*, to cause someone to adopt a different religion

myWorld Activity
To Dig or Not to Dig

Spanish Rule to Independence

In the late 1400s, explorers from Spain sailed to the Americas and began building colonies. The Spanish heard stories of a people—the Aztecs—who had large cities and vast amounts of silver and gold. The Spanish set out to find these people, leading to an encounter that changed the history of Mexico.

Arrival of Cortés In 1519, Spanish conquistador Hernan Cortés landed in Mexico. A **conquistador** is a soldier-explorer. The Aztecs greatly outnumbered Cortés and his 500 soldiers. Yet in just two years, Cortés defeated the Aztec Empire. Tens of thousands of Aztecs and their subjects died in the fighting.

Cortés destroyed Tenochtitlán and built Mexico City in its place.

Culture Change Under the Spanish, the lives of native peoples changed. Settlers from Spain and their descendants held the highest place in society. Native peoples had few rights. Priests came to Mexico to <u>convert</u> Native Americans to the Roman Catholic religion. The church became an important part of life in the new colony. Churches were built in the centers of towns and cities, and church officials became leaders in the colony.

Spain Struggles By the 1700s, Spain's empire had weakened. Spain's rulers decided to change the political and economic system to improve conditions in Mexico. They made new laws that led to increased trade. As Mexico's economy revived, Spain raised taxes and sent new officials to rule Mexico.

While Spain tried to improve Mexico,

COMMON MISCONCEPTIONS

Cinco de Mayo Many Americans think that the national holiday Cinco de Mayo is the Mexican independence day. This misconception may be due in part to the fact that, like the U.S. Independence Day celebrated on July 4, the Cinco de Mayo commemorates an important date in Mexico's history—May 5, 1862.

Mexico won independence from Spain some 40 years earlier, in 1821. The new government, however, faced many challenges, including an invasion by the French in 1861. When a French force of six thousand men attacked Puebla de Los Angeles, the inhabitants resisted and drove off the invaders. Although the French remained in Mexico for another five years, the victory on Cinco de Mayo is commemorated.

▲ After almost two years of fighting, the Spanish conquered the Aztecs. Soon after, the Aztecs were forced to become laborers.

▲ Spanish missionaries worked to convert native people to Christianity.

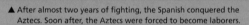

new ideas swept across Europe and the Americas. A movement called the Enlightenment questioned the rule of kings, and proposed that people had basic rights—rights that many in Mexico did not enjoy. People in North America acted on these ideas and declared independence from Great Britain. Their founding of the United States stood as an example to Spain's colonies.

Separating from Spain Early in the 1800s, the French emperor Napoleon Bonaparte invaded Spain. He named his brother Spain's new king. The French put a new person in control, who briefly ruled Mexico. In 1810, Mexicans launched a revolt that ended in 1821 with Mexico winning independence from Spain.

Reading Check How long did it take for Mexico to win independence?

Challenges for the Republic

While Mexicans had won independence, they faced new challenges. For many decades, their leaders struggled to solve the nation's problems.

Troubled Beginnings After the United States won independence, its new government struggled. In a few years, though, Americans wrote a new constitution that brought stability. The same did not happen in Mexico. The Mexican people did write a constitution, but different leaders competed for power. For the first few decades of Mexico's existence as a nation, they could not create a stable government.

In the middle 1800s, Benito Juárez became the leader of Mexico. He promised to make many changes that would help the nation's poor. Juárez

- **Cause and Effect** What Enlightenment idea strengthened Mexicans' desire for independence? (the idea that people have certain basic rights)
- **Cause and Effect** How did Mexico gain independence from Spain? (by winning a revolution)

Challenges for the Republic

- **Cause and Effect** What was the main cause of instability during the early years of Mexico's republic? (Leaders competed for power.)
- **Identify Main Ideas** What did Juárez hope to achieve? (help for the nation's poor)

READING CHECK 11 years

CORE CONCEPTS: FOUNDATIONS OF GOVERNMENT

Review Core Concept 8.1 before reading Constitution of 1917. Have students recall the definition of the term *constitution*. Discuss the desire of the Mexican people for a limited government, one that provides for people's needs. Ask students what the Mexican revolutionaries hoped the Constitution of 1917 would provide. (fair distribution of land)

GUIDE ON THE SIDE

Closer Look

Struggle for Power (continued)

- **Cause and Effect** Why did rich Mexicans seek help from France? (They wanted to retain their land.)

- **Summarize** How did Díaz try to build the nation's economy? (by inviting foreign companies to invest in Mexico)

- **Summarize** What did the Mexican Revolution hope to achieve? (political and social reform)

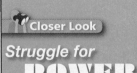

Closer Look

Struggle for POWER
continued

Colonial divisions between privileged Spanish and poor Native Americans caused tension. After independence, leaders like Porfirio Díaz made reforms, but problems remained. Widespread poverty led to revolution in 1910. By 1917, Mexico had its current constitution, which laid the groundwork for a more stable society.

THINK CRITICALLY How have gold, land, and oil created conflict in Mexico?

▲ Porfirio Díaz, upper left, encouraged economic growth using natural resources, like oil. Businesses prospered, but few shared in the wealth.

estate, *n.,* a large piece of land or property

promised to break up the large <u>estates</u> that the wealthy held and give some of this land to poor farmers.

Some Mexicans resented the changes Juárez made because they would lose wealth and power. They sought help from France. The French government sent an army that defeated Juárez. Then, France put an Austrian noble named Maximilian in control of Mexico. He tried to bring peace to the nation, but Juárez's supporters fought on. After several more years of fighting, Maximilian was overthrown. Back in power, Juárez was unable to make all the reforms he wanted.

Mexico under Díaz From the 1870s to 1911, Mexico's leader was Porfirio Díaz. At first, he tried to put in place many of the reforms of Juárez. He also tried to build Mexico's economy by inviting

foreign companies to build railroads and do other projects. Only a small number of Mexicans benefited, though. The great majority of people still lived in poverty. They worked long hours and had few rights and little food.

Mexican Revolution Unrest spread. Finally, in 1910, a candidate for president that Díaz supported lost the election to an opponent. Díaz had the opponent arrested and declared his man the winner. This action, along with Mexico's history of widespread poverty, sparked the **Mexican Revolution,** a period of armed rebellion in which Mexican people fought for political and social reform.

Constitution of 1917 The fighting eased in 1917, when a new constitution was declared. The new constitution made the government responsible for improving

THINK CRITICALLY Gold, land, and oil have created wealth for a minority, causing conflict between the rich and powerful and the poor.

READING CHECK Widespread poverty and a corrupt election caused the Mexican Revolution in 1910.

GOVERNMENT

Apostle of Democracy A proponent of democracy, Francisco Madero worked to end the dictatorship of Porfirio Díaz. In his 1908 book *The Presidential Succession in 1910,* Madero contended that Mexican presidents should be held to a single term. Using "Effective Suffrage—No Reelection" as his campaign slogan, Madero ran against Diaz in 1910. After being arrested the day before the election on apparently false charges, Madero fled to Texas, where he continued to stir up sentiment against Díaz.

Madero returned to Mexico and was elected president in 1911. However, he soon found himself in the middle of opposing political forces. A military coup led to his assassination in 1913. Nevertheless, Madero's democratic ideals, including fair elections and citizen participation in the political process, are said to have been a source of inspiration for Mexico's revolutionary forces.

GUIDE ON THE SIDE

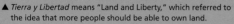

▲ *Tierra y Libertad* means "Land and Liberty," which referred to the idea that more people should be able to own land.

▲ The final panel shows foreign investors and the promise of Mexico's natural resources.

- **Identify Details** How does the mural reflect demands for reform? (Mexicans hold a banner demanding "Land and Liberty.")

- **Synthesize** What does the mural suggest about foreign influence? (It continues to play a major role in Mexico's economy.)

- **Draw Conclusions** Do you think that the Revolution improved the lives of Mexicans? Explain. (No, because the majority of Mexicans continued to be poor.)

Mexicans' lives. It declared the goal of giving land to poor farmers and more rights to workers.

Venustiano Carranza became president of Mexico but did not make many of the constitutional changes he promised. In a few years, leaders joined to overthrow him. In the next few decades, Mexico's leaders made some reforms, but the poor continued to suffer.

Reading Check What caused the Mexican Revolution in 1910?

Section 2 Assessment

? Essential Question

Key Terms

1. How did the Maya use their knowledge of astronomy?

2. What is a conquistador?

Key Ideas

3. What important role did the Olmecs play among Mexico's native peoples?

4. How did the development of Mexico's government differ from that of the United States?

5. What changes did the Constitution of 1917 promise to Mexico's people?

Think Critically

6. **Synthesize** What role did the Roman Catholic Church play in colonial Mexico?

7. **Draw Inferences** What details support the idea that the Mexican Revolution was not a complete success?

How much does geography shape a country?

8. How did Mexico's geography and the struggle for resources affect the history of Mexico? Go to your Student Journal to record your answer.

SECTION 2 ASSESSMENT **1.** The Maya used astronomy to develop calendar systems. **2.** A conquistador is a soldier-explorer. **3.** The Olmecs influenced later cultures. **4.** It took Mexico much longer to establish a stable government. **5.** The constitution promised to give land to poor farmers and more rights to workers. **6.** The Catholic Church assumed a role of leadership. **7.** Mexico's leaders did not reform society, and the poor continued to suffer. **8.** Mexico's limited farm land and other resources created struggle between the rich and the poor.

The Mexican Revolution

OBJECTIVES

Students will

- make connections between important documents and ideals of the Mexican Revolution.
- **21st Century Learning** draw conclusions about the success of the Mexican Revolution.
- **ELL** understand the terms *expropriated* and *proprietors*.

SET EXPECTATIONS

In this lesson, students will

- read and analyze two documents on resource distribution in Mexico.
- compare information in a contemporary news source to the content of the primary documents.

1 Connect

Have students think about what leads people to revolt. Brainstorm and then display possible reasons. Suggest that students think about why the American colonists revolted against England, such as to oppose high taxes, unjust laws, and limited freedom.

ELL **Early Advanced/Advanced** Ask volunteers to share information about causes of revolution, if relevant, in their home country. Lead students to conclude that revolution is directed against government.

2 Learn

Preview Have students preview the two pages and identify the images of Emiliano Zapata and modern-day farmers. Read the Key Idea, glossary terms, and definitions. Clarify any questions about the meaning of these words by providing examples. Read the introduction.

ELL **Advanced** Have students read to determine the nature of the property being discussed in the first document (land, water, timber). Then have them substitute *expropriate* and *proprietors* for the underlined words in the following sentence. <u>Seize</u> one third of the lands held by the wealthy <u>landowners.</u>

Read Slowly read aloud the excerpt from "The Plan of Ayala" without stopping. Read the document again, this time stopping to read the questions at the left. As you read each question,

prompt students to rethink and analyze the words. Have students use the location of the letters to provide clues to the answers. Do the same for the excerpt on land ownership in Mexico. Lead a discussion starting with students' responses to the questions. Ask, What does each document describe?

L2 **Extra Support** Post a table for students to use to compare the subject, point of view, and year written of the two documents.

 myWorld Activity: The Struggle Continues Distribute the *Activity Support: Newspaper Article Analysis*, through which students will analyze an excerpt from a contemporary newspaper article about the problems of today's Mexican farmers. Students will make connections to the documents in their text. **(Verbal/Logical)**

20 min

3 Understand

Review Go back to the Key Idea. Have students restate the economic plan proposed in "The Plan of Ayala." Discuss its likelihood of success.

Assess Have students complete **Analyze the Documents**. Review their answers to determine if they have met the lesson objectives. Post a simple

timeline on the board. Have the class list events before and after the Mexican Revolution.

Remediate Ask whether students think that people who are extremely poor are likely to be happy. Tell them to give reasons for their answer. Then have pairs of students share their ideas with each other.

Name _____ Class _____ Date _____

 myWorld Activity Support **Newspaper Article Analysis**

The Struggle Continues

Directions Read the excerpts below from a newspaper article. The article describes the way Mexican farmers feel about the removal of tariffs on imported corn and other agricultural products. (A tariff is a tax that raises the price of a product coming from another country.) Answer the questions that follow.

Mexican farmers protest end of corn-import taxes
By James C. McKinley, Jr.
Friday, February 1, 2008, *International Herald Tribune*

MEXICO CITY On Jan. 1, the last tariffs on corn, beans, sugar and milk were lifted under the North American Free Trade Agreement. . . . Since then, Mexican leaders of farm coalitions and other unionists have been calling for the government to renegotiate the treaty, putting them at odds with President Felipe Calderón, a staunch free-trade advocate.

The farmers worry that a surge of inexpensive corn could doom millions of peasants who farm plots of less than 12 acres. They also complain that the government has done almost nothing to prepare farmers for the open competition. . . .

"We are mostly angry with the Mexican government," said Victor Suárez, the leader of ANEC, a farmers' coalition. "They have left the small producers to fend for themselves."

Draw Conclusions

1. Why do you think it would be difficult for Mexican farmers to compete with American farmers?

_____

_____

2. Who do the Mexican farmers blame for their problems? How do their feelings relate to the feelings of Mexican revolutionaries?

_____

_____

_____

HISTORY

Land and Liberty Emiliano Zapata was a simple man who wanted justice for his people. Born in 1879, he worked tirelessly for land reform. *Tierra y Libertad,* meaning "Land and Liberty," became his slogan. Zapata created the "Plan of Ayala," a revolutionary document calling for redistribution of the land.

During the Mexican Revolution, Zapata became the leader of a guerilla force. Most of his "soldiers" were farmers who wore guns while working in their fields and who fought when called upon. Zapata worked throughout the war to implement fair land distribution and established Mexico's first credit organization for farmers. When Carranza, the leader of a rival faction, called a constitutional convention, he excluded Zapata. As a result, the "Plan of Ayala" was neither considered nor accepted.

GUIDE ON THE SIDE

Draw Conclusions Use the lettered prompts to help students draw conclusions and compare viewpoints expressed in documents written more than ten years apart.

ANSWERS

A Mexicans lack land for raising food. As a result, they are poor.

B Land would provide them with food and a means to make money.

C The Mexican poor will support it. The landowners will not.

Primary Source

The Mexican Revolution

Key Idea
- Leaders of the Mexican Revolution promised to relieve deep poverty by offering land to the poor.

Costumes for the anniversary of the revolution ▼

By 1910, a dictator named Porfirio Díaz had ruled Mexico for more than 30 years. Under Díaz, a small group of rich landowners controlled most of Mexico's land and wealth. Meanwhile, the majority of Mexicans were very poor. In 1911, Mexicans began a revolution. Soon, the revolutionaries broke into several groups. The leader of one group, General Emiliano Zapata, promised to take dramatic steps to help Mexico's poor. Fighting continued until 1920. Eventually a new constitution was written that promised reforms to help the poor.

Stop at each circled letter on the right to think about the text. Then answer the question with the same letter on the left.

A **Identify Main Idea and Details** What economic problems does the plan address?

B **Draw Inferences** Why did leaders of the revolution believe that owning land would improve conditions for Mexico's people?

C **Compare Viewpoints** How do you think the Mexican poor and the landowners would react to this part of the plan?

monopolized, *adj.,* held exclusively by a few

expropriated, *v.,* seized; taken

proprietors, *n.,* owners

Goals for a Second Revolution

[B]ecause lands, timber, and
A water are <u>monopolized</u> in a few hands, for this cause there will be <u>expropriated</u> . . . part of those monopolies from the powerful <u>proprietors</u> of them . . . in order that the pueblos and citizens of Mexico may
B obtain . . . fields for sowing and laboring, and Mexicans' lack of
C prosperity and well-being may improve in all and for all. "

— Emiliano Zapata, 1911, "The Plan of Ayala," in *Zapata and the Mexican Revolultion,* by John Warwick Jr.

Emiliano
Zapata

21st Century Learning DRAW CONCLUSIONS

To help your students draw conclusions and compare viewpoints, use the scaffolded questions that appear at the left of each excerpt. Encourage students to approach excerpts from primary sources in the same way that a scientist might examine a new discovery in minute detail. Students should understand each word and statement within the document before attempting to interpret the viewpoint of the writer. Once they arrive at an interpretation of each viewpoint expressed, students should be able to compare the two. For additional help, refer students to the **21st Century Online Tutor** *Draw Conclusions*.

GUIDE ON THE SIDE

Stop at each circled letter on the right to think about the text. Then answer the question with the same letter on the left.

D **Summarize** Why do the farm laborers have little freedom to leave?

E **Compare and Contrast** How does the life of peons in the 1920's compare to life before the Mexican Revolution?

F **Analyze Cause and Effect** What is the effect of this system on Mexican farm laborers?

peons, *n.,* workers of the hacienda

bondage, *n.,* slavery

haciendado, *n.,* owners of a hacienda, a large farm or ranch

meager, *adj.,* of small quantity

abject, *adj.,* reduced to the lowest level

George M. McBride on Land Ownership in Mexico, 1923

❝ The <u>peons</u> upon a Mexican hacienda are theoretically free. . . . As a matter of fact, however, many of them are held upon

D the estate in <u>bondage.</u> . . . By a system of advance payments, which the peons are totally unable to refund, the <u>haciendados</u> are able to keep them permanently under financial obligations and hence to oblige them to remain upon the estates to

E which they belonged. . . So <u>meager</u> is the compensation received by the peon that

F he is kept in the most <u>abject</u> poverty. ❞

—George M. McBride,
The Land Systems of Mexico, 1923

ANSWERS

D Farm laborers cannot leave because they owe money to the landowner.

E Technically the peons are free.

F The effect is to keep farm laborers in poverty.

Modern-day farmer working the land ▼

Analyze the Documents

1. **Draw Conclusions** How does the situation described in the second document compare to the economic complaint in the Plan of Ayala?

2. **Writing Task** Write a newspaper article from a 1920s viewpoint stating whether you think the Mexican Revolution was a success and explaining why or why not.

ANALYZE THE DOCUMENTS 1. Sample: The situation in the second document is very similar to the economic complaint in "The Plan of Ayala." Both documents describe Mexicans as poor. **2.** Sample: The Mexican Revolution was not a success. Many Mexicans are as poor today as were those who launched the Revolution. Land continues to be held by a wealthy minority while many Mexicans cannot feed their families.

Mexico Today

OBJECTIVES

Students will know

- the structure of Mexico's government.
- the effects of recent changes in the government, as well as current trends in education and the economy.

Students will be able to

- identify main ideas and details describing Mexico today.
- compare and contrast information relating to Mexico's economy.

SET EXPECTATIONS

In this section, students will

- read Mexico Today.
- choose to apply for one of two jobs in Mexico.
- go On Assignment in Mexico and learn more about life in San Nicolas Guadalupe, Mexico.

CORE CONCEPTS

You may wish to teach or reteach the following lessons from the Core Concepts Handbook:

- Trade, pp. 66–67
- Urbanization, pp. 80–81
- Conflict and Cooperation, pp. 110–111

KEY

Differentiated Instruction

- **L1** Special Needs
- **L2** Extra Support
- **L3** On-Level
- **L4** Challenge

English Language Instruction

- **ELL** Beginner
- **ELL** Early Intermediate
- **ELL** Intermediate
- **ELL** Early Advanced
- **ELL** Advanced

1 Connect
Make learning meaningful

Make Connections Begin the lesson by asking students to list ways in which family members help one another—with food, emotional support, and so forth. Ask students, How do you think family members continue to help each other even when they live far apart? Ask them whether they or anyone they know sends money to family members in another country. Discuss why people might need this extra help.

ELL Intermediate Point out that the term *remittance,* money sent to families abroad, includes the Latin root *mit* from the verb *mittere* meaning "to send." Help students apply this new information to other words such as *permit.*

Activate Prior Knowledge Remind students that in Section 2 they learned that the United States served as an example when Mexico sought independence. Ask them to predict how the government of Mexico might be similar to that of the United States.

L2 Extra Support Review the three branches of the United States government and the characteristics of a democracy.

Prepare Follow the steps in the section **Preview.** Preteach the Key Terms. Then have students complete *Word Wise* in their journals using in-text clues and the glossary for help.

2 Experience
Teach knowledge and skills

Read Use **Background** notes and **Guide on the Side** questions to model active reading. Have students use *Take Notes* in their **Student Journal** to identify main ideas and details about contemporary Mexico. Have students complete **21st Century Online Tutor** *Identify Main Ideas and Details,* and apply this skill to reading the section.

L1 Special Needs Post an agenda for the steps of the lesson so that students who need a high level of structure can know your plan ahead of time.

L4 Challenge Have students read *Enrichment: Biography of David Alfaro Siqueiros* to learn more about the role of political artists in Mexico.

ELL Intermediate Write *Agriculture, Manufacturing,* and *Services* on the board, translating as necessary. Have students identify images in the section that relate to each economic segment.

 Practice: myWorld Activity Students will compare and contrast help-wanted ads for jobs within two of Mexico's primary economic sectors. **Step-by-Step Instructions** and **More Activities** follow on p. T26.

SECTION 3 RESOURCE GUIDE

FOR THE STUDENT

my worldgeography.com Student Center

- Culture Close-up
- Data Discovery
- Active Atlas

Student Edition (print and online)

- Mexico Today

Student Journal (print and online)

- Section 3 Word Wise
- Section 3 Take Notes

21st Century Learning Online Tutor

- Identify Main Ideas and Details
- Compare and Contrast

FOR THE TEACHER

my worldgeography.com Teacher Center

- Online Lesson Planner
- Presentations for Projection
- SuccessTracker

ProGuide: Middle America

- Lesson Plan, pp. T24–T25
- 🏃 myWorld Activity Step-by-Step Instructions, p. T26
- Activity Support: Help-Wanted Ads, p. T27
- myWorld Geography Enrichment, p. T28
- Section Quiz, p. T29

Accelerating the Progress of ELLs

- Reading Support Strategies, p. 42

---

3 Understand
Assess understanding

Review Review *Word Wise* and *Take Notes* in the Student Journal.

Assess Knowledge and Skills Use the Section Assessment and Section Quiz to check students' progress.

Assess Understanding Review students' responses to the Section Assessment Essential Question prompt.

Remediate Use these strategies to review and remediate.

If students struggle to . . .	Try these strategies.
Recognize the three branches of government	Write the names of the branches on the board. Play a scenarios game that reviews which branch does what.
Evaluate the effects of free trade	Provide a math word problem about the price of American and Mexican corn before and after tariffs.
Differentiate between political parties	Complete a table as a class that includes comparisons of positions on trade, education, poverty, and crime.

ELL Support

ELL Objective Students will be able to use English to express cause-and-effect relationships.

Cultural Connections Have students use their home language to explain what causes people to migrate from their homeland to the United States. If they want to use English, provide the sentence structure, *"My family immigrated to the United States because _____."*

ELL Early Advanced Content Tip Have partners read Section 3 to identify the effect of the following: Constitution of 1917; the 2000 election; Mexican diversity; economic ties with the U.S.; NAFTA. Have them write a cause-and-effect sentence for each.

🏃 **ELL Activity** Show images of people working in agriculture or manufacturing. Have students choose a job and act out a related activity. Then have them write the English word for the job they chose and the verb that describes the action. **(Kinesthetic/Verbal)**

myWorld Activity | **Step-by-Step Instructions**

 30 min

Get a Job

OBJECTIVES

Students will

- compare and contrast want ads for jobs in Mexico.
- choose an advertised position.

LEARNING STYLE

- Verbal

21st Century Learning

- Compare and Contrast

MATERIALS

- Activity Support: Help-Wanted Ads, p. T27

Activity Steps

1. Tell students to imagine they are unemployed workers in Mexico. They have to choose which job advertised in their local paper to apply for.

   ELL Beginning/Early Intermediate Briefly review the meaning and conjugations of the verb *to work*. Also explain that people use the word *work* as a noun, like the word *job*, as in, "I need work" or "This is what I do for work. But *work* as a noun does not use an article where as *job* does—"I need *a job.*"

2. Allow time for students to read the two help-wanted ads on *Activity Support*. If students need more examples, bring in samples from online Mexican newspapers published in English.

3. Explain that help-wanted ads do not always provide complete information about an advertised job. Pay,

for example, is not always stated. Have students read the additional information under each want ad to help them make a decision.

4. Have students write a paragraph explaining why they would choose one job over the other. Tell them to include the positives and negatives of each position.

   L4 Challenge Have students research Mexico's economy to determine the fastest-growing sector and corresponding job opportunities. Have them give a brief report of their findings.

More Activities From myWorld Teachers

Local Connections Have partners research a local Mexican festival, such as the Day of the Dead or Cinco de Mayo, and then have them explain at least two customs related to the festival. **(Interpersonal)**

Gallery Mexico Present a slideshow of the paintings of Diego Rivera, Frida Khalo, and other Mexican artists. Have students identify aspects of the paintings that reflect European and Native American

traditions. Ask how the combination of cultures affects the paintings. **(Visual)**

Common Ground Have students explore similarities and differences between Mexico and the United States. Assign groups to create posters showing common ground or the lack thereof with regard to the economy, government, geography, and culture. **(Verbal)**

my worldgeography.com (**Teacher Center**) ➔ Find additional resources in the online Teacher Center.

Name _____ Class _____ Date _____

myWorld Activity Support   Help-Wanted Ads

Get a Job

Directions Suppose that you are looking for a job in Mexico. Read the following newspaper advertisements. Also suppose that you have learned additional information about each employer, which appears below each ad. Choose one of the jobs and write a paragraph explaining your choice. In your paragraph, explain the advantages and disadvantages of each position.

Help Wanted

> **Farm Workers Wanted** Farm workers wanted to pick, dry, and prepare coffee for shipping. Although this work is largely seasonal, a few reliable, productive workers may be hired full-time. Must be capable of steady physical labor. Pay is hourly, with a 35-hour minimum. We are a fair-trade farm.

Employer Information The farm has been owned and operated by the same family for three generations. For the last 10 years the coffee has been certified organic and fair trade.

> **Automobile Assembly Workers Wanted** Full-time assembly-line workers wanted to produce a new line of vehicles. Some overtime required during peak production periods.

Employer information The automobile company is owned by European investors. Overtime pay is the same hourly rate as regular full-time pay. Most managers and supervisors are Europeans, so there appears to be little opportunity for advancement.

Explain Your Choice Choose one of the advertised positions. Explain why you, an unemployed Mexican worker, made the choice that you did.

_____

_____

_____

_____

_____

Name _____ Class _____ Date _____

Enrichment: Biography of David Alfaro Siqueiros

Directions Read the selection below. Answer the questions that follow and complete the activity.

Born in 1896 in Chihuahua, Mexico, David Alfaro Siqueiros was a revolutionary artist in more ways than one. When he was a teenager, he traveled to Mexico City to study art. Before long, he had enlisted in the Revolutionary Army. From then on, his life was filled with political activism and artistic expression.

Siqueiros was a muralist whose work reflects the history and struggles of his people. *For the Complete Safety of All Mexicans at Work* is one example of how he expressed his concern for the worker through his art. Siqueiros also worked for fairness and safety in the workplace through his activities as a union organizer. His actions on behalf of indigenous people sometimes resulted in his arrest and imprisonment.

To paint his murals, Siqueiros often used industrial materials, such as paint spray guns. He sometimes used sculpture as well. In addition, Siqueiros painted on canvas. One of his best-known paintings is *Echo of a Scream*. Along with Diego Rivera and José Clemente Orozco, Siqueiros is known as one of "los tres grandes"—Mexico's three great muralists. He died in 1974.

1. How did Siqueiros's art show his beliefs?

_____

_____

2. Siqueiros believed that the work of the Mexican muralists had affected people throughout the world. How might people in other countries have been affected by their work?

_____

_____

Activity Work with your classmates to plan a mural in the tradition of Siqueiros. First, choose an issue of social justice, such as hunger or homelessness. Then decide what images to include in your mural. Sketch your mural on butcher paper.

Name _____ Class _____ Date _____

Section Quiz

Directions Answer the following questions using what you learned
in Section 3.

1. _____ Which statement about the
Institutional Revolutionary Party is correct?
   a. The Party consistently supported fair
   elections.
   b. The Party was in power for much of the
   1900s.
   c. The Party came to power in 2000.
   d. The Party nominated Vicente Fox for
   president.

2. _____ The National Action Party
   a. came into power in 1929.
   b. stands for one-party rule.
   c. is the party of President Felipe Calderón.
   d. opposed Vicente Fox.

3. _____ What has been the result of free-
market ideas in Mexico?
   a. greater economic growth
   b. less trade with other countries
   c. poor relations with the United States
   d. increased profits for small farmers

4. _____ What is the purpose of remittances?
   a. They may be used as travel vouchers.
   b. They are a type of passport.
   c. They are similar to food stamps.
   d. They increase a family's income.

5. _____ What is Race Day?
   a. an annual 5-kilometer run
   b. a celebration of Mexican culture
   c. a Native American celebration
   d. a national horse race

6. Provide the causes and the effects of each item listed in the diagram.

Causes	Effects
1999 political reforms _____ _____ _____	_____ _____ _____ _____
NAFTA _____ _____ _____	_____ _____ _____

Mexico Today

- Model preparing to read by previewing the Key Ideas, Key Terms, headings, visuals, and captions. Have students make predictions about what they will learn. For ELL support, post the prompt, "I predict I will read about . . ."

- Preview and practice identifying main ideas and details with a currently popular book, film, or television show.

- Preteach this section's high-use Academic Vocabulary using the table on the next page. Have students practice Academic Vocabulary and Key Terms by completing the *Word Wise* page in their journals.

GUIDE ON THE SIDE

Governing Mexico

- **Compare and Contrast** What type of government do Mexico and the United States have in common? (a federal republic)

- **Compare and Contrast** How is the structure of Mexico's government similar to that of the United States? (Its national government is divided into legislative, executive, and judicial branches.)

- **Sequence** How has the balance of power in Mexico's government changed in recent years? (Congress has gained more power.)

 Reading Skill

Identify Main Ideas and Details While they read, have students practice this skill by completing the *Take Notes* graphic organizer in the **Student Journal.**

Section 3

Mexico Today

Key Ideas
- Mexico has three branches of government. The Constitution of 1917 sets the framework for Mexico's government.
- Much of the Mexico's wealth is concentrated within a small upper class.
- Light manufacturing, natural resources, trade, and tourism support Mexico's economy.

Key Terms
- Institutional Revolutionary Party (PRI)
- National Action Party (PAN)
- free market
- remittance

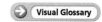 **Visual Glossary**

 Reading Skill: Identify Main Ideas and Details Take notes using the graphic organizer in your journal.

Voters participate in a recent election. ▼

The history of Mexico includes many struggles between rich and poor, as well as between native peoples and people of Spanish descent. Today, there are fewer struggles and Mexico's government is far more stable. The country's rich culture draws on the history of its diverse people. Mexico's economy continues to grow with increased manufacturing and trade. But the country still faces many social and economic challenges.

Governing Mexico

Mexico, like the United States, is a federal republic. A federal government shares power with state governments. Mexico has 31 states and a federal district. Since Mexico is a republic, its people elect their leaders. Those leaders then propose and enact laws.

Structure of Government Mexico's government has other similarities to the government of the United States. Mexico has a constitution. The Constitution of 1917 defines the structure of government, and states that all Mexico's people enjoy certain basic rights.

Mexico's national government is divided into three branches. The legislative branch creates laws. The executive branch, led by the president, carries out the laws. The judicial branch interprets the laws and decides whether actions of the other branches follow the constitution.

Mexico has a system of checks and balances between branches of government. The president has traditionally had more power than other branches, although Mexico's congress has gained more power recently.

ACADEMIC VOCABULARY

High-Use Word	Definition and Sample Sentence
dominate	*v.* to control or rule over *The visitor tried to dominate the conversation.*
dynamic	*adj.* active, or showing progress *The gymnast's performance was dynamic.*

GUIDE ON THE SIDE

Political Parties For many decades, a single political party <u>dominated</u> Mexico's government. That party is the **Institutional Revolutionary Party,** called the PRI after its name in Spanish. In 1929, the PRI gained control of Mexico's government. Every six years, the president would name another PRI member to succeed him, and that person would easily win the election.

In the late 1900s, many Mexicans voiced frustration over this one-party rule. They wanted to see more open elections, in the hopes that this change would produce better government. In 1999, President Ernesto Zedillo created some reforms. As a result, the 2000 presidential election was more fair than any earlier Mexican election. Candidate Vicente Fox, of the **National Action Party** (PAN), won the election.

Fair elections continued in later years. The PAN and other parties also gained more seats in Mexico's congress and in state governments. In 2006, Mexico's people elected another PAN leader, Felipe Calderón, president.

Citizens' Rights All Mexican people 18 or older have the right to vote in elections. Mexico's constitution actually requires people to vote in elections, although the law is not enforced.

Reading Check How did government in Mexico change in the 2000 election?

dominate, *v,* to control, or rule over

- **Identify Main Ideas** Why were many Mexicans dissatisfied with the PRI? (They wanted elections to be more open.)

- **Sequence** When did elections in Mexico start to become more fair? (in 2000)

- **Identify Main Ideas** Who has the right to vote in Mexico? (All Mexicans who are 18 or older.)

Analyze Visuals Have students compare and contrast the three images.

- How are the three images similar? (They all show Mexican presidents.)

- How are they different? (Calles was a PRI member. Fox and Calderón belong to the PAN.)

Mexican Politics, Then and Now

From 1929 to 2000, the Institutional Revolutionary Party (PRI) ruled Mexican politics. Presidents were often corrupt and made sure the person they picked won each election. In 2000, Vicente Fox became the first president who was not a member of the PRI.

Plutarco Calles made a "political machine" to ensure PRI victory.

Vicente Fox broke the 71-year rule of the PRI.

Felipe Calderón, of the PAN, won a close election in 2006.

READING CHECK The presidential election was more fair than previous elections and the PRI candidate was defeated.

ANSWERS

CULTURE

Fiestas Holidays in Mexico reflect the cultural blending that is characteristic of Mexico. Perhaps most remarkable is el Día de la Raza on October 12, the date on which Columbus arrived in the new world. Although his arrival resulted in great upheaval and historic change, Mexicans nevertheless choose to celebrate the rich diversity of their population on this day.

The holiday most associated with Mexico is el Día de los Muertos, or the Day of the Dead, celebrated at the end of October and the beginning of November. For centuries Mexico's indigenous people have followed this tradition of honoring their ancestors. Current celebrations incorporate elements of Catholic feasts. In 2003, el Día de los Muertos was chosen by UNESCO as a masterpiece of the oral and intangible heritage of humanity.

GUIDE ON THE SIDE

People and Culture

- **Compare and Contrast** How does the size of Mexico's Spanish-speaking population compare with that of other countries? (It is the largest in the world and nearly three times as large as Spain's.)

- **Identify Main Ideas** Which two groups make up the largest segments of Mexico's cultural and ethnic blend? (Spanish and Native Americans)

- **Identify Main Ideas** What modern art form has been traditionally practiced by Native Americans? (murals)

Analyze Visuals Have students read Blending Cultures and look at the images.

- What evidence of Spanish influence can they find? (celebration of Día de la Raza; mariachi bands)

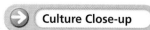

Culture Close-up

Have students visit myworldgeography.com to learn more about Mexico's culture.

People and Culture

With about 110 million people, Mexico is second in population only to Brazil among all Latin American countries. It has the largest Spanish-speaking population in the world—nearly three times more than Spain itself.

Cultures Blend Like many nations in the Americas, Mexico has a culture that blends, or mixes, traditions. Mexico's culture combines Spanish and Native American influences. In fact, about three out of five Mexicans have mixed Spanish and Native American ancestry. About one in three people is Native American. Most speak Spanish as well as their native language. Native Americans live mainly in southern Mexico. Many are Maya who live in the Yucatán Peninsula. Many members of another group, the Zapotecs, live in the Southern Highlands.

Mexicans honor mixed heritage on October 12. On this day—the Día de la Raza, or "Race Day"—Mexicans celebrate the contributions that all peoples have made to Mexican culture.

Mexico's art reflects its many cultures. Talented Mexican artists, following Native American tradition, have painted murals. These large-scale paintings are mounted on building walls and celebrate Mexico's history. Famous muralists include Diego Rivera and David Alfar Siqueiros. Another well-known Mexican artist, Frida Kahlo, painted self-portraits. José Clemente Orozco sculpted plaster.

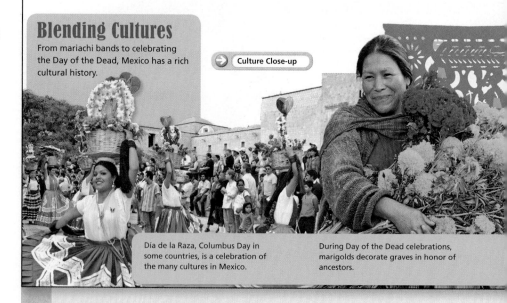

Blending Cultures

From mariachi bands to celebrating the Day of the Dead, Mexico has a rich cultural history.

Culture Close-up

Día de la Raza, Columbus Day in some countries, is a celebration of the many cultures in Mexico.

During Day of the Dead celebrations, marigolds decorate graves in honor of ancestors.

GEOGRAPHY

Sustainable Ranching Ranching is the primary economic activity in the Santa Cruz Valley in Mexico's northern Sonora region. Ranchers there have been working with U.S. ranchers along their common border to implement more sustainable land practices. Their efforts were initiated in 2003 by the Sonoran Institute, an organization that works to preserve Western Hemisphere lands.

Through the program's rancher-to-rancher exchange, Mexican and U.S. ranchers share land management techniques. Some Mexican ranchers have built small curtains of rock called gabions that reduce erosion by slowing down water flow in rivers and streams. The theory behind these efforts is that what is good for the land is ultimately good for both the cattle and the ranchers.

Religion The religious practices of Mexico's people also show the mixing of different cultures. About three quarters of the people practice the Roman Catholic faith. A growing number, though, belong to Protestant churches. This is especially true among poor people living in cities. Some Native Americans blend Christian and traditional beliefs, which is shown by celebrating the Day of the Dead.

Education Mexico's leaders have been working hard to improve education. The government has invested more in education by building schools, hiring teachers, and providing books and supplies. Today, about 91 percent of Mexicans over 15 can read and write. This is a sharp improvement since 1970.

Furthering their education will prepare Mexican children for the modern workplace. Increasingly, students in Mexico study English, which reflects continued economic ties between the United States and Mexico.

Still, education lags in rural areas, where some schools do not offer all grades. Many rural Mexicans move to cities to access better schools for their children. Students such as Carolina travel long distances to the schools they attend.

The government has tried to improve education for Native American children by providing textbooks and instruction in their native languages and in Spanish.

Reading Check What share of Mexico's population can read and write?

- **Synthesize** How would you describe religious diversity in Mexico? Explain. (Somewhat diverse; although 75 percent are Catholic, Protestantism is growing. Some Native Americans combine Christian and traditional beliefs.)

- **Compare and Contrast** How are schools most likely to differ between rural and urban areas? (City schools generally provide a better education.)

- **Identify Main Ideas** How is the government trying to improve education for Native American children? (by providing textbooks and instruction in their native languages and in Spanish)

People prepare hand-made goods for the Day of the Dead celebrations, including candy and paper flags, called papel picado (above).

Spanish mariachi bands play quick-tempo music in restaurants, festivals, weddings, and other gatherings throughout Mexico.

READING CHECK About 91 percent of Mexicans over 15 years of age can read and write.

ECONOMY

Shrimp Industry Grows Mexico's shrimp farming industry is one example of the country's increasingly diverse economy. The industry began relatively late, which has proved to be an advantage in that Mexican farmers have been able to learn from the experience of others. In Mexico, shrimp farmers are particularly diligent regarding the health of the shrimp they raise. In Sinaloa, for example, each sector of the state has

an aquatic health officer. This individual serves as a resource and also monitors farms to prevent the outbreak of disease within the stock.

The demand in Mexico for fresh shrimp is substantial, with Mexicans consuming 150,000 metric tons annually. As a result, Mexican shrimp farmers sell about 80 percent of their yield domestically. Most of what remains is sold to the United States.

Mexico's Economy

Cause and Effect

• What was the effect of tight government control of the economy during much of the 1900s? (The economy lagged.)

• What effect has adoption of free market ideas had on Mexico's economy? (growth and more jobs)

• **Summarize** What is NAFTA? (a free-trade agreement)

• **Identify Main Ideas** In what type of industry do the majority of Mexicans work? (service industries)

Chart Skills Point out the circle graphs.

• Which sector has shrunk the most relative to others? (agriculture)

➜ **Data Discovery**

Have students go to myworldgeography.com to learn more about Mexico's economy.

---

dynamic, *adj.,* active, or showing progress

Mexico's Gulf coast supports an active tourism industry. ▼

Mexico's Economy

Mexico has built a <u>dynamic</u> and growing economy. The nation now has one of the top economies in Latin America and one of the most productive economies in the world. For decades, Mexico depended on oil production to earn money while a large section of the population farmed. Now it has a more diverse economy.

Mexico's Economy at a Glance For most of the 1900s, Mexico's government tightly controlled the economy. The government owned some important enterprises, including the national oil company. It also put strict limits on other industries. As a result, economic growth lagged. In the late 1900s, leaders adopted **free market** ideas, which means the government took away

complex rules and let new companies compete. The result was more economic growth and more jobs.

Mexico has also built closer economic ties to the United States. In the 1990s, Mexico, the United States, and Canada signed NAFTA, the North American Free Trade Agreement. The three countries promised to take away rules that blocked trade between each other. For the most part, this meant taxes on goods that the countries traded with each other would be lower, so that goods could move between countries at a lower cost. As a result, trade with the United States has led to a growing Mexican economy, more manufacturing jobs, and increased pay for Mexican workers.

Mexico's Workers Approximately four out of six Mexican workers work in service industries. These industries include finance, communications, and healthcare. Tourism is an important service industry in Mexico too. Many people come from other countries to enjoy its beautiful resorts and the fascinating remains of its Native American cities. Another important service industry for Mexico is entertainment. Its television workers produce telenovelas, which tell complex stories with many characters. These long-running series delight not only Mexicans but people in other countries as well.

About one quarter of Mexican workers labor in factories. They process foods and make chemicals, iron and steel, cloth-ing, cars, and electronic goods. Some of the factories they work in are owned by foreign companies.

Mexico's Changing Economy

1950: Agriculture 19%, Industry 23%, Services 58%

2007: 4%, Industry 25%, Services 71%

■ Agriculture ■ Industry ■ Services

SOURCE: UN Economic Commission for Latin America and the Caribbean

Chart Skills

Since 1950, which sector has grown most?

➜ **Data Discovery**

CHART SKILLS the services sector

QUICK FACTS

Remittances After oil sales, remittances are Mexico's largest source of foreign income. However, Mexico's central bank reported that remittances in 2008 fell by 3.6 percent, the first annual drop since the bank began tracking remittances in 1995. This drop was likely due to a global financial crisis set off by the bust of the U.S. real estate market.

Mexicans living in the United States, many of whom work in construction, are particularly affected by construction and manufacturing declines. As a result, poor Mexicans living in both countries had even less to spend. Based on declining remittances and exports, Mexico's economy was projected to shrink by 1 percent in 2009.

Only four percent of Mexican people work on a farm. Some farmers grow cash crops such as coffee and fruits. Others tend the large herds of cattle that roam huge ranches in the north of Mexico. Many farmers, though, are among the nation's poorest people.

Some of Mexico's poor cannot find jobs in Mexico. They travel north to the United States to work. They send part of their earnings back home to support their families. These payments, called **remittances,** are an important part of

Mexico's economy. They help many poor families survive.

Mexico has a large share of young people in its population. They will be entering the workforce soon. The economy has to grow rapidly to provide enough jobs for all these new workers. If not, Mexicans will continue to leave the country looking for a place to work.

Reading Check Why do some workers leave Mexico for the United States?

myWorld Activity
Help Wanted: Mexico

The Remittance System in Mexico

A remittance is money earned in one country that is sent back to support families and others in a person's home country. The map below shows which Mexican states receive the most remittance money.

Map Skills

Region Where do most remittances go, to the north, to the south, or to central Mexico?

Active Atlas

KEY
Total Remittances to Mexico by State
Millions of dollars, 2006

- More than 1,500
- 851–1,500
- 501–850
- 251–500
- 25–250

▲ Higher wages in the United States create opportunity.

GUIDE ON THE SIDE

- **Identify Details** In what economic sector are workers most likely to be poor? (agriculture)

- **Cause and Effect** How will the economy affect young Mexicans if it fails to grow rapidly? (Many will not find jobs.)

Map Skills Point out the map of the remittance system.

- Why might the total amount of remittances be higher in some areas of Mexico than in others? (More Mexicans from those areas are sending money home.)

 myWorld Activity

Get a Job Find Step-by-Step Instructions and an Activity Support on pp. T26–T27.

Active Atlas

Have students visit myworld geography.com to learn more about Mexico's economy.

ECONOMICS

Trade Agreements According to the 2009 *CIA World Factbook*, Mexico's trade with the United States and Canada has nearly tripled since Mexico signed NAFTA in 1994. NAFTA, however, is only one of a dozen free-trade agreements entered into by Mexico with more than 40 countries. Its far-reaching agreements extend to Europe and Japan, as well as to the Central American countries of Guatemala, Honduras, and El Salvador. The combined effect of these agreements is that more than 90 percent of Mexico's trade now falls under the heading of free trade.

GUIDE ON THE SIDE

Closer Look

The Impact of Trade

- **Summarize** How is Mexico's economy becoming more diverse? (through production of more manufactured goods)

- **Cause and Effect** How has oil made Mexico's economy unstable? (Oil prices have changed.)

- **Analyze Charts** Which statistic in the bar graph indicates Mexico's economic reliance on the United States? Explain. (The United States purchases 82.2% of Mexico's exports.)

Closer Look

The Impact of Trade

In the 1990s, Mexico entered into the North American Free Trade agreement. While this agreement has led to more manufacturing jobs and increased trade, Mexico's economy is very dependent on the United States.

THINK CRITICALLY How does the amount of goods the United States buys affect Mexico's exports?

Mexican Exports

	Germany	Canada	United States
Percentage of Exports	1.5%	2.4%	82.2%

United States Exports

	China	Mexico	Canada
Percentage of Exports	5.6%	11.7%	21.4%

SOURCE: *CIA World Factbook*, 2008

Oil provided a base for Mexico's modern economy. Changing oil prices, however, made the economy unstable.

Many agricultural products, including coffee, fruits, and vegetables are shipped to the United States. Manufacturing goods, such as shoes and automobiles, has helped Mexico find other sources of income. This is known as diversifying an economy.

THINK CRITICALLY The amount of goods the United States buys increases Mexico's exports.

READING CHECK NAFTA is a free-trade agreement among the United States, Canada, and Mexico. It has allowed Mexico's economy to grow.

PRIMARY SOURCE

Small Farms, Big Challenges

"Not only are farmers not growing food, but we are going hungry because we can't afford the foreign food that drove us off our farms."

—A farmer in Oaxaca, Mexico from "As Food Prices Soar, Experts Debate Solutions" by David Koop

Farmers in Mexico are faced with fierce competition from NAFTA, as well as soil that is often unproductive. To help small farmers stay on their land, one group has reintroduced the milpa. This ancient farming technique involves the planting of three crops in the same plot: corn, beans, and squash. Together the plants naturally repel pests while at the same time enriching the soil. Yields, while small, have been enough to enable farmers to keep their land and feed their families.

Trade

Trade has become very important to Mexico's economy. Earnings from selling oil and oil products help finance the government. Manufactured goods and some crops are also major exports. Trade has brought many benefits—but also some problems.

Increased trade has allowed Mexico's economy to grow. Mexico belongs to the World Trade Organization (WTO), where it works with other countries to lower trade barriers. It has free trade agreements with more than forty other nations. Mexico's leaders hope to expand NAFTA to include more nations from Latin America in a zone called the Free Trade Area of the Americas (FTAA).

Providing Jobs Growing trade has led to more jobs in Mexico. However, Mexican workers earn less than those in the United States and Canada. Many manufacturers placed factories in Mexico to take advantage of lower wages.

Mexican workers make more than factory workers in China and other growing economies. Some Mexicans worry that more manufacturing jobs in China will lead to job loss in Mexico.

The Downside of Trade Dependence on trade has caused some problems, too. Some American companies have sold corn and apples in Mexico at lower prices than what Mexican farmers can afford to charge. As a result, Mexican farmers sell less.

Also, Mexico's great dependence on the United States means its economic success is closely linked to the United States economy. When the economy of the United States is doing well, Mexico benefits. When the United States economy slows down, Mexico also suffers. As a result, Mexico saw very slow economic growth in 2008.

Reading Check What is NAFTA, and how has it affected Mexico's economy?

IN NUMBERS
Mexico ranks **10th** in automobile manufacturing in the world. In 2007, Mexico produced more than **2** million vehicles.

Trade

Identify Details

- What aspect of trade helps to finance the government? (sale of oil and oil products)

- What are Mexico's major exports? (oil, manufactured goods, agricultural crops)

- **Draw Conclusions** Why do you think the government wants to expand the free-trade zone into Latin America? (to increase export opportunities)

- **Cause and Effect** How has competition affected Mexican farmers? (They are unable to compete with the low prices charged for some U.S. agricultural products.)

Section 3 Assessment

Key Terms
1. How did the Institutional Revolutionary Party stay in power for so long?
2. How are remittances important to Mexico?

Key Ideas
3. How does Mexico's Constitution of 1917 affect the government?
4. How has the government tried to improve education for Native Americans in Mexico?
5. What steps did Mexico's government take to change the economy starting in the 1990s?

Think Critically
6. **Identify Evidence** What are two examples of ways that Mexico reveals its blended culture?
7. **Draw Conclusions** What do the names of Mexico's political parties suggest about the goals of each party?

Essential Question

How much does geography shape a country?

8. How has Mexico benefited from having abundant deposits of oil? Go to your Student Journal to record your answer.

SECTION 3 ASSESSMENT **1.** controlled presidential elections **2.** They help poor families survive. **3.** It determines the government's structure. **4.** by providing textbooks and instruction in native languages **5.** elimination of complex rules to increase competition **6.** through art and celebration of Race Day **7.** Institutional Revolutionary Party: become an institution, or an integral part of the government; National Action Party: be an agent of change. **8.** Earnings from oil sales help finance the government and provide a base for Mexico's modern economy.

Mexico

Chapter Assessment

Key Terms and Ideas

1. **Recall** In what part of Mexico do **sinkholes** form?

2. **Explain** How does **irrigation** damage farmland?

3. **Compare and Contrast** What are the environmental differences between northern Mexico and southern Mexico?

4. **Sequence** Name the three major native Mexican civilizations in chronological order. Give the name of the **conquistador** who brought about the end of the native empires.

5. **Describe** What was life like for the natives during Spanish rule?

6. **Synthesize** What is the difference between the war for independence in 1810 and the **Mexican Revolution** that occurred in 1910?

7. **Explain** Why do some Mexicans go to the United States in order to send **remittances** to their families?

8. **Discuss** What recent changes have occurred in the Mexican economy, and have they resulted in economic improvement?

Think Critically

9. **Identify Evidence** Of which resources are Mexicans making good use and which resources do they need to develop further?

10. **Make Inferences** What were the problems caused by the PRI party holding power in Mexico for more than 70 years?

11. **Predict** What would happen to the Mexican economy if tourism dropped dramatically?

12. **Core Concepts: People's Impact on the Environment** What environmental problems will Mexico face during the next 10 years?

Places to Know

For each place, write the letter from the map that shows its location.

13. **Yucatán Peninsula**
14. **Sierra Madre Occidental**
15. **Mexico City**
16. **Mexican Plateau**
17. **Rio Grande River**
18. **Merida**
19. Using the scale, estimate the distance between Mexico City and Merida.

Mexico: Cities and Features

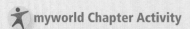 **myworld Chapter Activity**

A Time for Judgment Find Step-by-Step Instructions, Student Instructions and Rubric, and an Activity Support on pp. T5–T7. **(Verbal/Logical/Interpersonal)**

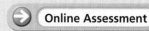 **21st Century Learning**

Analyze Media Content Students' explanations should compare the contents of the three articles chosen, pointing out any elements of bias. If students need help with this skill, direct them to the online tutorial *Analyze Media Content*.

→ **Online Assessment**

Tailor review and assessment to each student's needs with an array of online assessments.
• Self-Test
• On Assignment Article or Slideshow
• Success Tracker

? Essential Question
myWorld Chapter Activity

Judging Mexico's Leaders Assess the achievements of Mexico's leaders, including Montezuma, Cortés, Maximilian, Juarez, Zapata, and Calderón. Judge whether or not the leaders met their goals for Mexico and analyze the effects of the leaders' success or failure on Mexican history.

21st Century Learning
Analyze Media Content

Find three articles online about the presidential race in 2006, between Felipe Calderón and Andrés Manuel López Obrador. Analyze the articles. Is there evidence of bias, or a favoring of one view over another? Does the article suggest the election results were fair? Do supporters of Obrador or Calderón feel the results were fair? Explain your answer.

WRITING TASK TIP

Use Data Remind students that information may appear in more than one form. Demonstrate how to correlate information contained in writing with data that appears in a graph or table. Post an example, such as "Ninety percent of our family's food is purchased. The rest is home grown." Then have students display the information in a graph or a table.

Document-Based Questions

Success Tracker™
Online at myworldgeography.com

Use your knowledge of Mexico and Documents A and B to answer Questions 1–3.

Document A

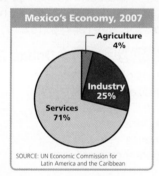
Mexico's Economy, 2007
- Agriculture 4%
- Industry 25%
- Services 71%
SOURCE: UN Economic Commission for Latin America and the Caribbean

Document B

" The mountains here are rugged and difficult, so that they can hardly be crossed, even on foot. Twice I have sent people to conquer them, but they have never been able to do anything against these Indians, who are well armed and entrenched in their mountains."

—Hernando Cortés to Charles V, 1526

1. What kind of work do most Mexican people do for a living?
   A Most people work in agriculture.
   B More than half of the people work in either agriculture or industry.
   C Most people work in the service areas of the economy.
   D More people choose to work in industry than in the service areas of the economy.

2. What was the advantage the Aztecs had that Cortés described to Charles V?
   A The Aztecs were familiar with the territory.
   B Aztec weapons were superior to Spanish weapons.
   C The Aztecs built camps in the mountains.
   D The Spanish were outnumbered.

3. **Writing Task** What does the description Cortés gives of Mexico's landscape suggest about the availability of farmland?

DOCUMENT-BASED QUESTIONS

1. C
2. C
3. Cortes's description of a mountainous landscape suggests that the availability of farmland is limited. This corresponds to the data in the graph in Document A, which shows that fewer people are employed in agriculture than in other economic sectors.

Central America and the Caribbean
CHAPTER RESOURCE GUIDE

Plan With Understanding by Design

Chapter Objectives
Begin With the End in Mind

Students will demonstrate the following enduring understandings:
- Geographic factors create socio-economic challenges.
- Different political and economic systems have varying effects on national stability and quality of life.
- There are both benefits and drawbacks of international involvement for small nations.

Connect
Make Learning Meaningful

Student Edition
- **Essential Question** Is it better to be independent or interdependent?
- **myStory** Luis shows tourists a way to appreciate natural beauty without harming wildlife.

my worldgeography.com
myStory Online Get to know Luis through a video of his life and home.

Student Journal
Essential Question Preview

Experience
Teach Knowledge and Skills

Student Edition
- Read Sections 1, 2, and 3.
- Answer Reading Checks and Section Assessment questions.

my worldgeography.com
On Assignment Visual Glossary, Active Atlas, Data Discovery, Language Lesson, Culture Close-up, and Self-Test

Student Journal
- Sections 1, 2, and 3 Word Wise
- Sections 1, 2, and 3 Take Notes

Teacher's Edition
myWorld Activities
- Section 1: Location Equation, p. T38
- Section 2: Corners of History, p. T44
- Section 3: Is Free Fair?, p. T52

21st Century Learning Online Tutor
- Use Parts of a Map
- Synthesize
- Analyze Cause and Effect
- Make Decisions
- Summarize
- Compare Viewpoints

Understand
Assess Understanding

Assessment Booklet
- Chapter Tests   • Benchmark Tests

Teacher's Edition
myWorld Chapter Activity
Students will create business plans for new tourism development and compete for funding.

Success ☆ Tracker™
Online at myworldgeography.com
Administer chapter tests and remediate understanding.

my worldgeography.com
On Assignment Students will write an article or create a multimedia presentation about the region's independence from, and interdependence with, other countries.

Student Edition
Chapter Assessment

Student Journal
Essential Question Writer's Workshop

Connect to the Essential Question

Essential Question

Is it better to be independent or interdependent?

Use the Essential Question poster and follow these steps to help students understand the Essential Question.

Connect to Their Lives

1. Have students think of an area in their lives in which they are able to act on their own. (If students have already studied this Essential Question, encourage them to think of new examples.) What do they like about being independent? What do they dislike about it?

2. Have students think of an area in their lives in which they must depend on others. What do they like about being interdependent, and what do they dislike about it?

3. Post the following table for them to complete or have students turn to the *Essential Question Preview* page in their **Student Journals.**

	Advantages	Disadvantages
Independence		
Interdependence		

Connect to the Content

4. Now have students name areas in which countries act independently and areas in which countries act interdependently. Point out that some areas, such as fighting a war, can be done either independently or interdependently, depending on the circumstances.

5. Post the following chart on the board. Have students use it to record their ideas about areas of national independence and interdependence.

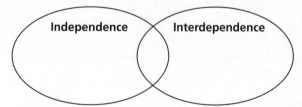

6. After previewing the chapter, have students make chapter-related predictions on the *Essential Question Preview* page in the **Student Journal.**

7. Remind students that they will answer a prompt related to the Essential Question on each section's *Take Notes* page in the **Student Journal.**

Explore my worldgeography.com

Welcome to myWorldGeography

http://www.myworldgeography.com

ON ASSIGNMENT: Central America and the Caribbean

For this chapter's assignment, students will
- take a digital trip to the countries of Central America and the Caribbean.
- take on the role of a journalist.
- gather notes, images, and data for their story throughout their journey.
- write an article or create a multimedia presentation connecting the collected data and images to this chapter's Essential Question: *Is it better to be independent or interdependent?*

ITINERARY

During their trip, students will make the following stops:

 myStory Video

Learn more about how Luis helps his family and works toward a better future.

 Active Atlas

Read more maps of Central America and the Caribbean.

 Data Discovery

Gather data from more charts about life and the economy in the region.

 Culture Close-up

Check out what life was like on a historic sugar plantation.

 Language Lesson

Learn to say "Hello," "Thank you," and more in Spanish.

 Self-Test

Assess their own knowledge of chapter content.

While on their trip, students will practice the following skills:
- **Analyze** characteristics of regional cultural diversity
- **Evaluate** the extent of political and economic interdependence within a global context

TIGed
TakingITGlobal for Educators

Extend the reach of every lesson by helping students connect to a global community of young people with common interests and concerns. Visit myworldgeography.com to
- explore Country Pages relating to Central America and the Caribbean.
- delve deeper into this chapter's Essential Question, *Is it better to be independent or interdependent?*
- find online alternatives to and solutions for the Unit Closer Activity.

 worldgeography.com

TEACHER CENTER

Preview and assign student materials, enrich your teaching, and track student progress with the following resources:
- Online Lesson Planning and Resource Library
- Presentations for Projection
- Online Teacher's Edition and Ancillaries
- Google Earth Links

Assess Enduring Understandings

 myWorld Chapter Activity   **Step-by-Step Instructions**   **2 hr**

Venturing in Nicaragua

Teach this activity at the end of the chapter to assess enduring understandings.

OBJECTIVES

Students will demonstrate the following enduring understandings:

- Geographic factors create socioeconomic challenges.
- Different political and economic systems have varying effects on national stability and quality of life.
- There are both benefits and drawbacks of international involvement for small nations.

Students will provide the following evidence of understanding:

- Tourism Business Plan
- Presentation of Business Plan

LEARNING STYLES

- Logical   • Visual   • Verbal

MATERIALS

- Activity Support: Student Instructions and Rubric, p. T34
- Activity Support: Business Plan, p. T35
- Activity Cards: #19–24
  19. Tourism Businesses in Nicaragua
  20. Environments Attracting Tourists
  21. Natural Disasters
  22. Perspectives on Tourism
  23. Tourist's Map of Nicaragua
  24. Efforts to Promote Tourism

Activity Steps

1. **Set Expectations** Tell students they will be taking on the role of tourism developers in Nicaragua. They will compete for investment money from a major Nicaraguan bank, but the bank's loan officer (you) will only grant one loan. Teams will select a location and a type of tourism business, describe its potential benefits to the community, and address any potential risks or opposition. Review with students *Activity Support: Student Instructions and Rubric* on the following page.

   ELL Early Intermediate/Intermediate Help students understand the meaning of *development* in economic terms. For example, show photos of a store's grand opening.

2. **Research** Divide the class into teams of four to five students. Set up six stations with one Activity Card at each. Have students do research to develop their plan. Rotate teams through the six stations. Students should focus on the following questions. They can record ideas on *Activity Support: Business Plan*.

- Where should they locate their business and why?
- What kind of business should they start? Why did they choose that kind?
- Who might oppose their business plan?
- What environmental risks might there be?

3. **Finalize Plans** Have each team decide on a location and type of business based on their research. Tell half of each team to draft a description of the business and its benefits (profits, jobs, services). Tell the other half to draft an explanation of potential opposition and risks.

4. **Present Plans** Have students present their plans to you and the class with notes on chart paper, electronically, or in a loan interview.

5. **Assess** Using the rubric on the following page, have students assess their own plans and presentations. Assess each team's attainment of the enduring understandings of this chapter. Report to each team whether their plan will be funded and why.

Name _____ Class _____ Date _____

Venturing in Nicaragua

Activity Instructions Read the following summary of your myWorld Chapter Activity. Follow your teacher's directions for more information.

1. Work with your development team to conduct research using your book and the Activity Cards. Use information from the chapter and the cards to plan a new tourism business in Nicaragua. Try to research answers to these questions:

   a. Where should you locate your business and why?

   b. What kind of tourism business should you start? Why?

   c. Who might oppose your business plan?

   d. What environmental risks might there be?

2. Select a location and a type of tourism business.

3. Create a plan describing the business and its possible benefits.

4. Create a list of potential risks and opposition. Describe your response to each.

5. Present your plan to your teacher (the loan officer) and the class in competition for a business loan.

myWorld Chapter Activity Rubric	3 Exceeds Understanding	2 Reaches Understanding	1 Approaches Understanding
Research	Uses information from all three sections, more than three cards, and two online features	Uses information from at least three cards and one other source	Uses information only from the cards
Business plan	Describes with detail more than three benefits and responds to more than three risks	Describes with detail at least three benefits and responds to at least three risks	Describes with detail fewer than three benefits and fewer than three risks
Presentation and collaboration	Every team member participates in explaining the plan.	Most members participate in explaining the plan.	One or two members participate in explaining the plan.

Name _____ Class _____ Date _____

myWorld Chapter Activity Support   Business Plan

Venturing in Nicaragua

Directions Use this page to take notes on important information and ideas that you will use to craft a tourism business plan for a location in Nicaragua. Then brainstorm the benefits and risks that would come with your business.

Location	Types of Business

Location _____

Description of Business

_____

_____

_____

Benefit	Risk	Response to Risk

Central America and the Caribbean

- Introduce the Essential Question so that students will be able to understand the big ideas of this chapter (see earlier page, Connect to the Essential Question).

- Help students prepare to learn about Central America and the Caribbean by looking at the chapter's maps, charts, and photos.

- Have students make and record chapter predictions with the *Essential Question Preview* in the **Student Journal.**

- Ask students to analyze the map on this page.

GUIDE ON THE SIDE

Explore the Essential Question . . .

Have students complete the Essential Question Writer's Workshop in their **Student Journal** to demonstrate in-depth understanding of the question in the context of this chapter.

Analyze Maps Point out the political map.

- Which two Caribbean nations share the same island? (Haiti and the Dominican Republic)

- Between what two bodies of water do the countries of Central America lie? (the Pacific Ocean and the Caribbean Sea)

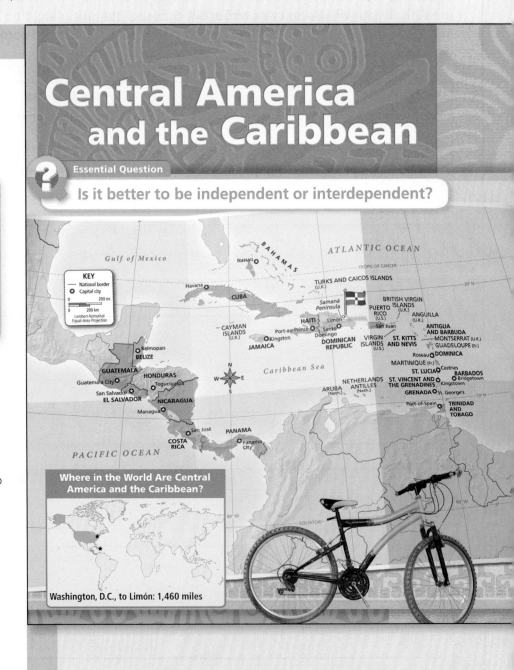

Central America and the Caribbean

Essential Question

Is it better to be independent or interdependent?

KEY
— National border
✪ Capital city

0   200 mi
0   200 km
Lambert Azimuthal
Equal-Area Projection

Gulf of Mexico · ATLANTIC OCEAN · BAHAMAS · Nassau · TROPIC OF CANCER · Havana · CUBA · TURKS AND CAICOS ISLANDS (U.K.) · Samaná Peninsula · PUERTO RICO (U.S.) · BRITISH VIRGIN ISLANDS (U.K.) · ANGUILLA (U.K.) · HAITI · Limón · San Juan · ANTIGUA AND BARBUDA · CAYMAN ISLANDS (U.K.) · Port-au-Prince · Santo Domingo · VIRGIN ISLANDS (U.S.) · ST. KITTS AND NEVIS · MONTSERRAT (U.K.) · GUADELOUPE (Fr.) · Kingston · DOMINICAN REPUBLIC · JAMAICA · Roseau · DOMINICA · MARTINIQUE (Fr.) · ST. LUCIA · Castries · BARBADOS · Bridgetown · Belmopan · BELIZE · Caribbean Sea · NETHERLANDS ANTILLES (Neth.) · ST. VINCENT AND THE GRENADINES · Kingstown · GRENADA · St. George's · GUATEMALA · HONDURAS · ARUBA (Neth.) · Guatemala City · Tegucigalpa · Port-of-Spain · TRINIDAD AND TOBAGO · San Salvador · EL SALVADOR · NICARAGUA · Managua · San José · PANAMA · COSTA RICA · Panama City · PACIFIC OCEAN

Where in the World Are Central America and the Caribbean?

EQUATOR

Washington, D.C., to Limón: 1,460 miles

NOTES

INTRODUCE **my Story**

Get students excited to learn about Central America and the Caribbean by first experiencing the region through the eyes of Luis, a young man from the Dominican Republic.

• Read myStory and watch the myStory Video about his life.

• Have students complete *Working for the Future* in the **Student Journal** to prepare to learn about life in Central America and the Caribbean.

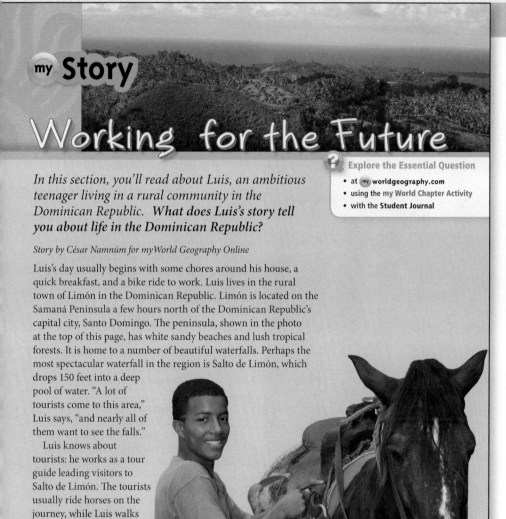

my Story

Working for the Future

 Explore the Essential Question
• at **my worldgeography.com**
• using the **my World Chapter Activity**
• with the **Student Journal**

In this section, you'll read about Luis, an ambitious teenager living in a rural community in the Dominican Republic. What does Luis's story tell you about life in the Dominican Republic?

Story by César Namnúm for myWorld Geography Online

Luis's day usually begins with some chores around his house, a quick breakfast, and a bike ride to work. Luis lives in the rural town of Limón in the Dominican Republic. Limón is located on the Samaná Peninsula a few hours north of the Dominican Republic's capital city, Santo Domingo. The peninsula, shown in the photo at the top of this page, has white sandy beaches and lush tropical forests. It is home to a number of beautiful waterfalls. Perhaps the most spectacular waterfall in the region is Salto de Limón, which drops 150 feet into a deep pool of water. "A lot of tourists come to this area," Luis says, "and nearly all of them want to see the falls."

Luis knows about tourists: he works as a tour guide leading visitors to Salto de Limón. The tourists usually ride horses on the journey, while Luis walks on foot to guide them.

GUIDE ON THE SIDE

my Story

Working for the Future

• **Identify Details** In what country does Luis live? (the Dominican Republic)

• **Identify Details** What is Luis's job? (tour guide)

 On Assignment

Have students go to myworldgeography.com to receive their assignments from a virtual newspaper editor. Students will explore Central America and the Caribbean to better understand Luis's story and the key ideas of the chapter.

QUICK FACTS

Work in the Dominican Republic Agriculture was once the main sector of employment in the Dominican Republic. Today, however, tourism is one of many service industries that together employ more than 63 percent of the labor force. Unemployment in the Dominican Republic is high, with a 2008 estimate of 15.4 percent. Approximately 40 percent of the population lives below the poverty line.

GUIDE ON THE SIDE

- **Infer** Why might it be more difficult to climb the mountain during the rainy season? (The ground is more likely to be slippery.)

- **Draw Conclusions** Why is protecting the environment important to the Dominican economy? (The region's natural beauty draws tourists.)

Salto de Limón drops 150 feet into a deep pool of water.

Luis guides tourists on horseback.

Walking with tourists to a waterfall may sound like a simple job, but it is not. Visitors to the falls must climb up a steep trail for more than an hour to reach Salto de Limón. It can be a dangerous hike during the rainy season, when the trail is wet and slippery. But Luis has made this trip more than 200 times, and he knows the way well. When he was a child, he and his friends came here to swim and hunt for fresh fruit. Now Luis is almost 17 years old, and he enjoys taking tourists to this special place.

The natural beauty of the Samaná Peninsula makes it very popular with tourists. As a result, the government and the region's people are working to protect the waterfalls and the surrounding area. A local group of tourism-based businesses helps encourage the protection of natural resources and the environment.

In Limón, Luis lives with his grandmother, Doña Graciela, and a few brothers and cousins. "My mother has been in Puerto Rico for

Luis's cousins

ECONOMICS

Ecotourism With its natural beauty, biodiversity, and tropical location, the Dominican Republic is a popular tourist destination. Its many and diverse ecological zones offer a wide range of activities. Visitors to Salto de Limón, for example, ride horses—perhaps guided by Luis—in order to reach a swimming hole at the base of a spectacular waterfall.

In winter, thousands of humpback whales winter in Samaná Bay, where they attract enthusiastic whale watchers. Birders travel to view some three hundred species—twenty-seven of which are found only on Hispaniola.

Luis lives with his grandmother.

Luis enjoys a meal with his family.

Attending school is very important to Luis.

eight years and my uncle lives in New York," he says. "My grandmother raised me."

Luis thinks of himself as an ordinary teenager. He begins a typical day by doing housework and shopping for groceries. "After my chores I like to go bike-riding," Luis says with a smile. He usually rides the mile or so to work, where he meets tourists ready to travel to Salto de Limón.

When Luis returns from leading a tour group to the falls, he is hot, tired, and often covered with mud. Then he gets ready to go to school in the afternoon. Not all Dominican children his age attend school, but Luis thinks it is important. "I want to finish my studies and get my worker's permit so I can work in the city," he says. Getting a work permit would lead to many opportunities for Luis. He wants to earn enough money to provide for his family, and he would love to be able to visit his mother in Puerto Rico.

Because it is not always tourist season in Limón, Luis also does chiripeos, or side jobs around town. Sometimes he works at construction sites. At harvest time, he helps the owner of a small organic coffee plantation pick and dry coffee beans. And, he adds, "Sometimes I go with my cousin to help with his grandmother's conuco." A conuco is a small plantation where families grow crops for their own use. Luis helps take care of the crops. Sometimes there are crops left over to sell, and Luis is able to make extra money.

No matter where you find Luis, one thing is clear: he is an extremely hardworking young man with a very bright future.

 myStory Video

Join Luis as he shows you more about his life in the Dominican Republic.

Meet the Journalist

Name César Namnúm
Favorite Moment Seeing Luis's energy and determination

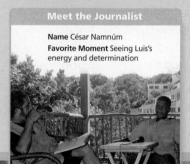

- **Compare and Contrast** How is Luis different from others his age? (He has the opportunity to go to school.)
- **Identify Details** How does Luis divide his day? (among work, school, and family)
- **Summarize** In addition to guiding tourists, what else does Luis do to earn money? (He sometimes works on construction sites, helps with the coffee harvest, and sells surplus crops from his family's plot.)

myStory Video

Have students watch the video at myworldgeography.com about Luis's life working in the village where his family lives. Tell students to use their trackers to collect images and data about life in the Caribbean.

Chapter Atlas

OBJECTIVES

Students will know

- regional biodiversity and natural disasters.
- economic importance and environmental hazards of tourism and agriculture.

Students will be able to

- identify and locate major physical and political features of the region on a map.
- describe the relationship among climate, land use, and biodiversity.

SET EXPECTATIONS

In this section, students will

- read Central America and the Caribbean.
- make connections between ecosystems, land use, and natural disasters.
- go On Assignment in Central America and collect information about life in the region.

CORE CONCEPTS

You may wish to teach or reteach the following lessons from the Core Concepts Handbook:

- Forces Inside Earth, pp. 24–25
- Climate and Weather, pp. 32–33
- People's Impact on the Environment, pp. 52–53

KEY

Differentiated Instruction		English Language Instruction		
L1 Special Needs	**L2** Extra Support	**ELL** Beginner	**ELL** Early Intermediate	**ELL** Intermediate
L3 On-Level	**L4** Challenge	**ELL** Early Advanced	**ELL** Advanced	

1 Connect
Make learning meaningful

Make Connections Ask students to think about the climate extremes of their region. Have them identify extremes like drought, earthquakes, floods, etc., and describe how these extremes affect people's lives in their area. Have students write in their journal about what they would normally do on the hottest and the coldest days of the year.

L1 Special Needs Play a recording of a local forecast for severe weather. Ask students to compare the severe weather and the typical weather of their region.

Activate Prior Knowledge Remind students that in the previous chapter they learned about Mexico's varied landscape. Ask them to predict some characteristics that Central America and the Caribbean might share with Mexico. Ask what kinds of plants and animals they would expect to find.

L2 Extra Support Review the visuals in myStory. Ask students to describe the location and what they already know about tropical places.

Prepare Follow the steps in the section **Preview.** Preteach the Key Terms. Then have students complete *Word Wise* in their journals using in-text clues and the glossary for help.

2 Experience
Teach knowledge and skills

Read Use **Background** notes and **Guide on the Side** questions to model active reading. Have students use *Take Notes* in their **Student Journal** to label the outline map of the region. Have students complete **21st Century Online Tutor** *Use Parts of a Map* and apply this skill to reading the section.

L1 Special Needs Have students read the **Online Student Edition** while listening to the accompanying audio.

ELL Beginning Have students make flashcards for basic place vocabulary (river, mountain, sea, forest, grass, etc.) with definitions and translations plus a specific example from the chapter. For example, for "mountains," students would note "Pico Duarte" and its location.

L4 Challenge Have students research a tropical plant that is common to the region—for example, orchids—and determine where in the region it would most likely thrive and why.

 Practice: myWorld Activity Students will use manipulatives to match a location, land use, and potential natural disaster in order to explain relationships between the environment and human activity in the region. **Step-by-Step Instructions** and **More Activities** follow on p. T38.

SECTION 1 RESOURCE GUIDE

FOR THE STUDENT

my worldgeography.com Student Center
- Active Atlas
- Data Discovery

Student Edition (print and online)
- Chapter Atlas

Student Journal (print and online)
- Section 1 Word Wise
- Section 1 Take Notes

21st Century Learning Online Tutor
- Use Parts of a Map
- Synthesize

FOR THE TEACHER

my worldgeography.com Teacher Center
- Online Lesson Planner
- Presentation for Projection
- SuccessTracker

ProGuide: Middle America
- Section 1 Lesson Plan, pp. T36–T37
- myWorld Activity Step-by-Step Instructions, p. T38
- Activity Support: Matching Squares, p. T39
- myWorld Geography Enrichment, p. T40
- Section Quiz, p. T41

Accelerating the Progress of ELLs
- Reading Support Strategies, p. 42

---

3 Understand
Assess learning

Review Review students' work in their **Student Journal.**

Assess Knowledge and Skills Use the Section Assessment and Section Quiz to check students' progress.

Assess Understanding Review students' responses to the Section Assessment Essential Question prompt.

Remediate Use these strategies to review and remediate.

If students struggle to . . .	Try these strategies.
Describe regional ecosystems	Replay the myStory Video and review characteristics of a tropical forest.
Identify what causes physical geography to change	Point out and discuss the photo showing the aftermath of a hurricane.
Comprehend *biodiversity*	Help students to break the term into two parts, bio- and diversity. Talk about what each part means. Compare the *biodiversity* of a city block to the rainforest.

ELL Support

ELL Objective Students will be able to use English to name and describe ecosystems.

Cultural Connections Have students name natural disasters their families or friends have experienced or that they know about. Let them use both English and their native language.

ELL Intermediate Content Tip Use the visuals in Core Concepts Lesson 3.6 to review types of ecosystems and the words used to categorize ecosystems: rainfall, temperature, plant life, and animals. Explain that some of the ecosystems discussed in this section do not appear in the world map because they are smaller ecosystems within larger regions.

ELL Activity Distribute photos of the region's ecosystems. Post a chart of the various systems and have students place photos under the appropriate heading. Have volunteers add to the display by drawing additional characteristics. **(Visual/Kinesthetic)**

my worldgeography.com Lesson Planner

myWorld Activity **Step-by-Step Instructions**

  20 min

Location Equation

OBJECTIVES

Students will

- make connections between location, land use, and environmental hazards.
- synthesize information in order to make choices.

Activity Steps

1. Distribute copies of *Activity Support: Matching Squares*. Have students read the instructions and then cut out the nine squares using scissors.

2. Ask students to pick one location square, one land-use square, and one natural disaster square that, when combined, seem plausible in real life in Central America or the Caribbean.

3. Have pairs of students share their combinations and explain why they believe those cards fit together in a manner that models a real location in the region. Students can also record their explanations on the activity support.

   L1 Special Needs If students struggle to use scissors, have them use a pen or pencil to draw a line connecting the squares they wish to combine.

LEARNING STYLE

- Logical
- Visual

21st Century Learning

- Synthesize

MATERIALS

- scissors
- Activity Support: Matching Squares, p. T39

4. Then ask students to speculate about the impact of the natural disaster on the economic activity they chose. Have students record their speculation on the activity support.

   ELL Beginner Provide students with cards that say "before" and "after.". Say the words to the students, and have them repeat. Have them cut out or draw pictures of places before and after a natural disaster and place the pictures next to the right word.

5. Poll the class to see how many students combined the same cards. Have them explain their choices to the whole class.

6. (Optional) Have students do further research to confirm if their combinations and speculations were accurate for the region.

More Activities From myWorld Teachers

Local connections Ask students to act out two sides of a debate on a proposed development project in their area that poses environmental risks. **(Verbal/Logical)**

First Responder Have students design emergency survival kits for earthquakes, volcanic eruptions, and hurricanes. **(Logical)**

Help Wanted Have students make job advertisements for an industry specific to a given area, such as for a sugarcane worker in the Dominican Republic or a bauxite miner in Jamaica. **(Visual/Verbal)**

 my worldgeography.com Teacher Center → Find additional resources in the online Teacher Center.

Name _____ Class _____ Date _____

 myWorld Activity Support   **Matching Squares**

Location Equation

Directions Below is a grid with three columns of information: three different locations, three different ways to use the land, and three different natural disasters. All these examples could occur in Central America and the Caribbean. Cut out the nine squares and make a set of one location, one land use that would be likely in that place, and one natural disaster that might happen in that location. Be prepared to explain why you chose your set.

Location	Land Use	Natural Disaster
tropical rainforest	textile factory	earthquake
savanna/grasslands	tourism	hurricane
highlands	banana or sugar plantation	volcanic eruption

Answer the following questions about your choices.

1. Explain why you feel these three characteristics could explain a real event in the region.

_____

_____

2. What effect would the natural disaster have on the location and the economic activity you chose?

_____

_____

Name _____ Class _____ Date _____

Enrichment: Earthquakes in El Salvador

Directions Read the selection below. Then answer the questions that follow.

El Salvador has a history of severe earthquakes. The earthquakes are due to the motion of the Cocos Plate, a tectonic plate that is moving the Pacific Ocean floor northeast toward the El Salvador coast.

Earthquakes vary in strength and in amount of destruction. Scientists measure earthquakes on what is called the Richter Scale. Stronger earthquakes receive higher numbers. For example, an earthquake that measures 4 on the Richter Scale is ten times as strong as an earthquake that measures 3. Earthquakes over 5 on the Richter Scale can cause a significant amount of damage to buildings. They can even cause mudslides where the soil is lacking roots to hold it in place.

In poor countries, like El Salvador, where many families live in homes made with weak materials and simple structures, an earthquake can easily flatten homes and cause deaths. In rural, hilly areas, where most trees have been cut down to clear space for crops, earthquakes can cause mudslides that can carry away livestock, people, and houses. People living in crowded, badly constructed apartment complexes in cities like San Salvador, the capital of El Salvador, can also easily become victims of earthquakes.

Major Earthquakes in El Salvador since 1950		
Date	**Magnitude**	**Fatalities**
May 6, 1951	6.2	400
May 3, 1965	6.3	125
October 10, 1986	5.5	1000
January 13, 2001	7.7	852
February 13, 2001	6.6	315

Source: U.S. Geological Survey

1. Which earthquake had the strongest magnitude? _____

2. During which year did earthquakes cause the greatest loss of life? How might an earthquake with the lowest magnitude also cause the most deaths?

_____

_____

Name _____ Class _____ Date _____

Section Quiz

Directions Answer the following questions using what you learned
in Section 1.

1. _____ Another term for "isthmus" is
   a. lowlands.
   b. mangrove forest.
   c. highlands.
   d. land bridge.

2. _____ What causes hurricanes to form in
   Central America and the Caribbean?
   a. trade winds
   b. extreme heat
   c. lack of cloud cover
   d. drought

3. _____ One example of biodiversity is
   a. cattle ranching.
   b. the variety of living things in coral reefs.
   c. an increase in the strength of hurricanes.
   d. sugar plantations.

4. _____ Tourism is most essential to the
   economies of which two island nations?
   a. the Bahamas and Jamaica
   b. Haiti and the Bahamas
   c. Haiti and Jamaica
   d. Dominican Republic and Haiti

5. _____ One effect of deforestation is
   a. soil enrichment.
   b. loss of wildlife habitat.
   c. increase in native medicinal plants.
   d. increase in bird populations.

6. Complete the table below to show the negative effects of cattle
   ranching, tourism, and deforestation on the region's environment.

Cause	Effect on Environment
Cattle ranching	
Tourism	
Deforestation	

Chapter Atlas

- Model preparing to read by previewing the Key Ideas, Key Terms, headings, visuals, and captions. Have students make predictions about what they will learn. For ELL support, post the prompt, "I predict I will read about . . ."

- Preview and practice the reading skill, label an outline map, by drawing and labeling maps of their own neighborhoods.

- Preteach this section's high-use Academic Vocabulary and Key Terms using the table on the next page and in-text definitions. Have students practice Key Terms by completing the *Word Wise* page in their journals.

GUIDE ON THE SIDE

Physical Features

- **Categorize** Which land masses does Central America connect? Which oceans does it separate? (North and South America; Atlantic and Pacific)

- **Identify Details** What are the three largest islands of the Caribbean? (Cuba, Jamaica, Hispaniola)

Reading Skill

Label an Outline Map While they read, have students identify the Places to Know! on the outline map of the region in the **Student Journal.**

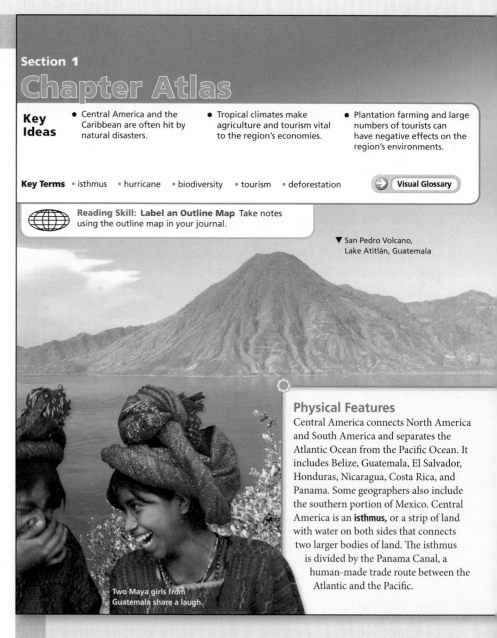

Section 1
Chapter Atlas

Key Ideas
- Central America and the Caribbean are often hit by natural disasters.
- Tropical climates make agriculture and tourism vital to the region's economies.
- Plantation farming and large numbers of tourists can have negative effects on the region's environments.

Key Terms • isthmus • hurricane • biodiversity • tourism • deforestation

○→ **Visual Glossary**

🌐 **Reading Skill: Label an Outline Map** Take notes using the outline map in your journal.

▼ San Pedro Volcano, Lake Atitlán, Guatemala

Two Maya girls from Guatemala share a laugh.

Physical Features
Central America connects North America and South America and separates the Atlantic Ocean from the Pacific Ocean. It includes Belize, Guatemala, El Salvador, Honduras, Nicaragua, Costa Rica, and Panama. Some geographers also include the southern portion of Mexico. Central America is an **isthmus,** or a strip of land with water on both sides that connects two larger bodies of land. The isthmus is divided by the Panama Canal, a human-made trade route between the Atlantic and the Pacific.

ACADEMIC VOCABULARY

High-Use Word	Definition and Sample Sentences
major	*adj.* of great importance *The election of a president is a major political event.*
dense	*adj.* crowded *Populations in rural areas are not as dense as those in cities.*

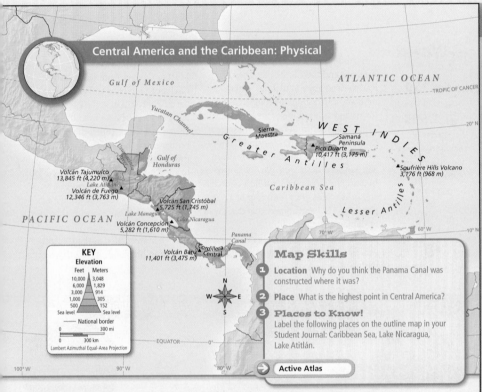

Central America and the Caribbean: Physical

Gulf of Mexico

ATLANTIC OCEAN

TROPIC OF CANCER

Yucatan Channel

Sierra Maestra

W E S T   I N D I E S

Samaná Peninsula

Pico Duarte 10,417 ft (3,175 m)

Soufrière Hills Volcano 3,176 ft (968 m)

Greater Antilles

Gulf of Honduras

Volcán Tajumulco 13,845 ft (4,220 m)

Lake Atitlán

Volcán de Fuego 12,346 ft (3,763 m)

Volcán San Cristóbal 5,725 ft (1,745 m)

Caribbean Sea

Lesser Antilles

Lake Managua

Lake Nicaragua

Volcán Concepción 5,282 ft (1,610 m)

Panama Canal

PACIFIC OCEAN

Volcán Barú 11,401 ft (3,475 m)

Cordillera Central

KEY
Elevation

Feet	Meters
10,000	3,048
6,000	1,829
3,000	914
1,000	305
500	152
Sea level	Sea level

National border

0   300 mi
0   300 km

Lambert Azimuthal Equal-Area Projection

EQUATOR

Map Skills

1. **Location** Why do you think the Panama Canal was constructed where it was?

2. **Place** What is the highest point in Central America?

3. **Places to Know!**
Label the following places on the outline map in your Student Journal: Caribbean Sea, Lake Nicaragua, Lake Atitlán.

 Active Atlas

To the east of Central America are the Caribbean Sea and hundreds of islands. Cuba, Jamaica, and Hispaniola are the largest Caribbean islands. Many smaller islands were formed by volcanoes.

Several mountain ranges divide the region. The Caribbean's highest peak is Pico Duarte in the Dominican Republic. Mexico's Sierra Madre mountains extend south into Guatemala, El Salvador, and Honduras. Some of the mountains of the Sierra Madre are high enough to be covered with snow in winter. In Panama, the Cordillera Central mountain range divides the western and eastern parts of the country. Precipitation in the Central American highlands forms important lakes and rivers, such as Lake Atitlán and the Usumacinta River.

The slow but steady movement of plates below Earth's surface makes this region physically unstable. The Central America and the Caribbean region has more than eighty active volcanoes. Volcán de Fuego in Guatemala is perhaps the most active. The Soufriere Hills Volcano in Montserrat had a <u>major</u> eruption in 1997. Today much of Montserrat is closed to people and more than half of its population has moved away.

major, *adj.,* of great importance

MAP SKILLS 1. The Panama Canal was built at the shortest distance between the Pacific Ocean and the Caribbean Sea. **2.** Volcán Tajumulco **3.** Students should correctly label the Caribbean Sea, Lake Nicaragua, and Lake Atitlán on their maps.

GUIDE ON THE SIDE

- **Identify Details** What is the Caribbean's highest mountain peak? (Pico Duarte)

- **Draw Conclusions** Why does Central America have so many active volcanoes? (The movement of Earth's plates causes volcanic activity.)

- **Cause and Effect** Why have so many people moved away from Montserrat? (There is an active volcano on the island.)

Analyze Visuals Have students compare the countries of Central America with those of the Caribbean.

- On what type of landform are the Caribbean nations located? (islands)

- What is the landform on which Central America rests? (isthmus)

Active Atlas

Have students go to myworldgeography.com to view more maps of Central America and the Caribbean.

GEOGRAPHY

A Caribbean Jewel Renowned for its beauty and biodiversity, the Mesoamerican Reef is the largest barrier reef in the Western Hemisphere. Nearly 450 miles long, the reef supports habitat for many species, including 60 species of coral, 350 species of mollusk, and 500 species of fish.

Threatened species of turtles and manatees, among others, live in habitats associated with the reef. The many threats to this haven of biodiversity include coastal development, pollution, overfishing, and oil spills.

GUIDE ON THE SIDE

Climate and Life

- **Summarize** How does Central America's location affect its climate? (Because it is near water and the equator, it is warm and wet.)

- **Compare and Contrast** How do patterns of precipitation differ in low-lying coastal areas as compared to the highlands? (In the lowlands it rains all year. The highlands have a dry season and a rainy season.)

- **Cause and Effect** Why does much of Central America's population live in the highlands? (The climate is better suited for growing a variety of crops.)

Analyze Visuals Indicate the map and have students analyze it.

- What type of vegetation covers most of Central America and the Caribbean? (forest)

21st Century Learning

Use Parts of a Map Have students develop this skill by using this interactive online tutorial and activities. Students will learn to use parts of a map to better understand a region's geography.

my World IN NUMBERS

About **750** species of trees and **1,500** species of flowering plants live in 4 square miles of tropical rain forest.

Earthquakes are common in Central America and the Caribbean. They can lead to dangerous mudslides, when mud and earth slide down hillsides onto towns and cities in lower areas. The city of San Salvador in El Salvador has been destroyed by earthquakes—and rebuilt—several times. In 2001 an earthquake in San Salvador destroyed 100,000 homes. In Antigua, Guatemala, roofless churches and other ruins are a reminder of a powerful 1773 earthquake that destroyed or damaged many buildings.

Reading Check What makes Central America and the Caribbean physically unstable?

Climate and Life

Most of Central America and the Caribbean region is wet and warm because the region is close to large water bodies and the Equator, or 0° latitude. Warm east winds called the trade winds bring rain to the region. These year-round rains provide water for forests and tropical crops like bananas and coffee. When the trade winds form powerful rainstorms, they become known as **hurricanes,** or intense storms that form over the tropical Atlantic Ocean.

Higher areas such as the Central American highlands have a dry season

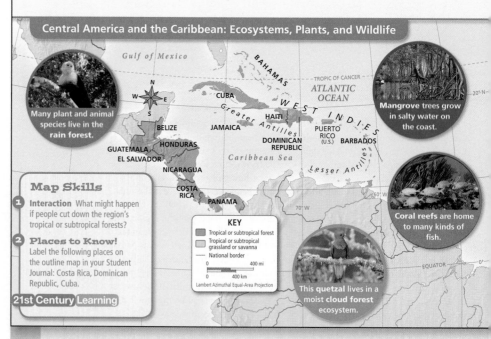

Central America and the Caribbean: Ecosystems, Plants, and Wildlife

Many plant and animal species live in the **rain forest.**

Mangrove trees grow in salty water on the coast.

Coral reefs are home to many kinds of fish.

This **quetzal** lives in a moist **cloud forest** ecosystem.

Map Skills

1 **Interaction** What might happen if people cut down the region's tropical or subtropical forests?

2 **Places to Know!** Label the following places on the outline map in your Student Journal: Costa Rica, Dominican Republic, Cuba.

21st Century Learning

KEY
- Tropical or subtropical forest
- Tropical or subtropical grassland or savanna
- — National border

0   400 mi
0   400 km
Lambert Azimuthal Equal-Area Projection

READING CHECK the movement of Earth's plates

MAP SKILLS 1. loss of wildlife habitat **2.** Students should correctly label Costa Rica, Jamaica, and Cuba.

QUICK FACTS

The Strength of a Storm Hurricanes fall into one of five categories, with a Category 1 hurricane being the weakest and a Category 5 the strongest. In Category 1, a hurricane typically would sustain winds of between 74 and 95 miles per hour, cause minimal damage to infrastructure, and result in a storm surge of between 4 to 5 feet. A Category 5 hurricane would have winds of more than 155 miles per hour, destroy buildings, and produce a storm surge of more than 18 feet.

---

and a rainy season. The area's mountains block the trade winds, leading to less rain in the winter months. The lack of rain between December and April can lead to water shortages. As a result, these areas cannot support tropical forests. They are, however, suitable for cattle ranching.

The Central American highlands have a relatively <u>dense</u> population. Most people in Central America live in the highlands because of the dry, cool highland climate. This climate allows people to grow a variety of crops.

Caribbean countries have generally lower elevations. Their climates are similar to the lower areas of Central America.

Due to the region's warm, wet weather, tropical and subtropical ecosystems cover Central America and the Caribbean. Tropical rain forests cover most areas that have not been cleared of trees. Tropical grasslands have formed in regions where people have cut down rain forests. Some countries, such as Costa Rica, have a rare ecosystem called cloud forest. Cloud forests are higher and cooler than lowland forests, with moist clouds that are near the ground. They support diverse wildlife.

Most Caribbean islands are surrounded by an underwater ecosystem known as coral reef. Reefs are largely made up of tiny organisms—coral—that produce a substance similar to limestone as they grow. Over time, coral reefs become large underwater islands that are home to a wide variety of tropical fish and other marine life. This variety of living things is called **biodiversity**.

Reading Check What is an underwater ecosystem common in the Caribbean Sea?

Hurricane Havoc

The region's unique ecosystems, warm days and nights, and beautiful beaches attract visitors from many parts of the world. However, the region's powerful hurricanes can cause great damage and keep visitors away.

Residents of Caribbean islands and coastal countries like Honduras face an average of eight hurricanes a year. Hurricanes usually occur in summer and early fall. These storms can bring several inches of rain an hour, as well as powerful 150-mile-per-hour winds that can harm many people and destroy entire towns.

myWorldActivity
Location Equation

dense, *adj.,* crowded

Hurricanes can cause serious damage in the region. ▼

Hurricane Damage

Hurricane Ike
Year: 2008
Deaths: 7
Damages: $4 billion

Hurricane Mitch
Year: 1998
Deaths: 6,500 (approx.)
Damages: $4 billion

Hurricane Ivan
Year: 2005
Deaths: 39
Damages: $815 million

BAHAMAS
ATLANTIC OCEAN
CUBA
Greater Antilles
HAITI DOMINICAN REPUBLIC
BELIZE
JAMAICA
PUERTO RICO (U.S.)
Lesser Antilles
GUATEMALA
HONDURAS
WEST INDIES
Caribbean Sea
EL SALVADOR NICARAGUA
BARBADOS
GRENADA
COSTA RICA
PACIFIC OCEAN
PANAMA
90°W   60°W   10°N
0   300 mi
0   300 km
Lambert Azimuthal Equal-Area Projection

READING CHECK coral reef

Hurricane Havoc

- **Identify Details** When are hurricanes most likely to occur? (summer and fall)

- **Cause and Effect** What are some of the effects of hurricanes? (People are injured. Towns can be destroyed. Tourism suffers.)

Analyze Visuals Have students compare the information on the three hurricanes shown.

- Which hurricane had the greatest effect? Explain. (Hurricane Mitch caused the greatest number of deaths and the most damage.)

- Within how long a period of time did the three major hurricanes occur? (ten years)

myWorld Activity

Location Equation Find Step-by-Step Instructions and an Activity Support on pp. T38–T39. **(Logical/Visual)**

ECONOMICS

Sustainable Farming Finca Buenos Aires, a coffee farm in Guatemala, is a sustainable farm. There, owner Felipe Guzmán grows coffee under the forest canopy's shade. Instead of spraying pesticides to control harmful beetles on the farm's 182 acres, Guzmán breeds wasps that attack the beetles' larvae. To help prevent erosion and water pollution, areas of natural forest border the farm's springs and rivers.

Sustainable practices have earned Finca Buenos Aires certification as a sustainable farm by the Rainforest Alliance. By using such practices, even large farms can minimize their impact on the environment.

GUIDE ON THE SIDE

Land Use

- **Identify Details** What mineral is important to the economy of Jamaica? (bauxite)

- **Compare and Contrast** How do most people in in rural and urban areas make their living? (rural areas: farming; urban areas: commerce and manufacturing)

Analyze Maps Have students look at the map to compare ways in which the region uses land.

- Where is land used the least for agriculture? (urban areas)

- Why would the brown-shaded areas be the least productive for farming? (They are mountainous.)

Active Atlas

Students may visit myworldgeography.com for more maps of the region.

my World IN NUMBERS

Costa Rica is the world's leading producer of pineapples, growing more than **9** million metric tons of pineapples a year.

Recently, hurricanes have become stronger and more frequent. Some scientists believe that this change is due to higher air and sea temperatures, also known as climate change, or global warming.

Hurricanes threaten people's safety and cause widespread destruction. Strong hurricanes, such as Hurricane Ike (2008) and Hurricane Mitch (1998), have damaged the region's roads, farms, schools, and businesses. Countries often depend on help from foreign countries and international aid groups like the International Red Cross and Red Crescent Movement to rebuild after hurricanes.

Reading Check How do hurricanes affect Central America and the Caribbean?

Land Use

Despite environmental dangers like hurricanes and earthquakes, the region's people still find ways to live off the land. But the countries in Central America and the Caribbean are small compared to countries in North or South America. Due to their relatively small sizes, these countries have few natural resources.

Common Land Uses Most Central Americans in rural areas are farmers. Those in urban areas work in commerce and manufacturing. Mining is a land use in some countries. In Jamaica, bauxite is mined for making aluminum. The region produces some petroleum, but most countries must import oil.

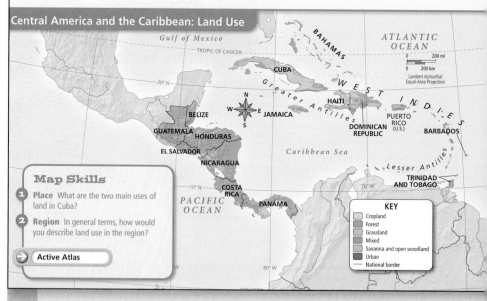

Central America and the Caribbean: Land Use

Map Skills

1 **Place** What are the two main uses of land in Cuba?

2 **Region** In general terms, how would you describe land use in the region?

Active Atlas

READING CHECK Hurricanes threaten people's safety and damage the infrastructure.

MAP SKILLS 1. cropland, forest **2.** agricultural and rural, few large cities

CULTURE

Crop Over Cultural traditions originate from many sources, including the harvesting of crops. One such example is the Crop Over festival in Barbados. This festival originally celebrated the completion of the sugarcane harvest. Although the harvest celebrations eventually died out, Crop Over was reborn as a music festival in the 1970s. Today Crop Over is a celebration of calypso, traditional foods, and the arts. The festival ends with the Grand Kadooment, a parade featuring bands in costume.

Warm temperatures and fertile soil make large-scale agriculture possible in the lowlands of Central America and the Caribbean. Plantations, or large commercial farms, grow cash crops such as sugar or coffee. Cash crops are usually sold to other countries rather than sold locally. In fact, much of the food eaten in the region is imported from other countries.

When farmers do have small plots of land to grow their own crops, they keep what they need for their families and sell the surplus, or what is left over, at local markets. In places where it is too dry to grow many crops, ranchers raise livestock, particularly cattle. Cattle ranching, however, employs relatively few workers. It can also cause environmental problems, such as erosion, which is the removal of soil by wind or water.

Tourism Tourism is one of the most important land uses in Central America and the Caribbean. **Tourism** is the business of providing food, places to stay, and other services to visitors from other places. It is the fastest-growing part of the Caribbean economy.

The Bahamas and Jamaica have two of the region's largest tourist-based economies. Tourists spend money while they shop and see sights. They go scuba diving on coral reefs and hiking in rain forests. Cruise ships and resorts employ many local workers. However, these jobs usually pay local workers very little. Foreign companies and investors make most of the profit earned from tourism.

Reading Check Name three ways that the region's people live off the land.

The region's beaches and other natural features attract many tourists, who often outnumber the year-round population.

Chart Skills

1. About how many times larger is the number of tourists that visit Antigua and Barbuda in one year than the number of people who live there?

2. What do you think are the benefits and drawbacks of having more foreign visitors than year-round residents?

Data Discovery

Key

= 10,000 people

Barbuda
Antigua
Year-round Residents = 83,000

Barbuda
Antigua
Foreign Visitors = 239,000

**Antigua and Barbuda
Tourist versus Year-round Population, 2005**

SOURCE: UN Population Division and UN World Tourism Organization

ANSWERS

PRIMARY SOURCE

Reefs in Danger "Unless the world gets serious about reducing greenhouse gas emissions in the next few years, it is likely there will be massive bleaching and deaths of corals around the world . . . This will have significant impacts on the lives of the people . . . who are dependent on reefs for food, for tourism, and for protecting the land they live on."

—Clive Wilkinson, global coral authority and coordinator of the Global Coral Monitoring Network "Report: 20% of World's Corals Already Dead," Underwater Times.Com, December 10, 2008

GUIDE ON THE SIDE

Environments in Danger

- **Synthesize** Why does tourism sometimes create water shortages? (Tourists increase the demand for water.)

- **Cause and Effect** How do sugar and coffee plantations affect the amount of food available in the Caribbean and Central America? (So much land is used for these products that there is not enough land to raise food.)

Closer Look

Crops and Water Pollution

- **Sequence** How do pesticides and chemicals move from farms to the sea? (Rain washes them into rivers; rivers carry them to coastal waters.)

- **Draw Conclusions** Who is most likely to benefit from large-scale farming? Who is most likely to lose? (owners of large farms; all those who depend on clean water, as well as those who fish and work in ecotourism)

- **Analyze Visuals** If large-scale farming continues, do you think it will benefit or harm the region's economies? Explain. (Some may say that the economic benefits outweigh the disadvantages. Others may say that the negative environmental impact and reduced tourism will be very costly.)

Environments in Danger

While people depend on the land for food and energy, they sometimes harm the very environments they need to survive. Some people question whether tourism is the best way to use land. The presence of many tourists increases the population density, which can make life more difficult for local people. Water shortages are common, particularly in busy tourist areas like Jamaica or during the dry season of popular tourist regions in Costa Rica.

Pollution Large-scale farming can have environmental consequences. Most small countries in the region grow cash crops such as sugar or coffee to export to other countries. Pesticides and chemicals used to grow large amounts of a single crop can pollute the water supply. Water pollution can kill plants and animals, harming ecosystems such as coral reefs. This decreases biodiversity, one of the region's main tourist attractions.

Pollution also contaminates commercial fishing areas, killing fish. This is a

Closer Look

Crops and Water Pollution

The economies of small countries in the region often depend on a few cash crops, such as corn and sugar cane. Many large farms use chemicals called pesticides to kill organisms that harm crops. But pesticides can also harm humans, plants, and animals. Rain can wash pesticides into streams and rivers. This water pollution—called runoff—travels downstream to oceans, killing coral reefs and fish.

THINK CRITICALLY How could pollution from pesticide runoff affect coastal economies?

A sugar plantation in Barbados

Farmers apply pesticides to protect crops.

When it rains, pesticides wash off crops and flow into rivers.

Rivers carry pesticides through many different habitats.

Toxic waters drain into the ocean.

Pesticides can kill marine life and harm ecosystems.

ANSWERS

THINK CRITICALLY Pesticide runoff will poison fish and affect the livelihood of fishers. It will harm coral reefs and pollute coastal waters, which will negatively affect tourism.

READING CHECK Deforestation causes soil to erode and become dry. It also causes the people or animals that lived in that forest to no longer have a home. Sometimes it might mean that important medicines from plants are lost.

HISTORY

Old World Ancestors Although jaguars are only found in the Western Hemisphere, they are descendants of Old World cats. Their ancestors crossed the Bering Strait from Asia and gradually moved into Central America.

Unlike other large cats, jaguars are good swimmers and often live near water. They are capable of a number of vocalizations, including a roar that sounds like a deep cough.

Jaguars once roamed as far north as New Mexico and as far south as Argentina. Today, due to hunting and loss of habitat, the jaguar is an endangered species. The spotted cat lives in Central and South American pockets of tropical forest.

major concern for countries that engage in commercial fishing for export, such as Belize and Honduras.

Deforestation Before large numbers of people occupied the region, tropical forest covered most of the land. Centuries later, ranching, farming, and the need for timber led to **deforestation,** or the clearing of large numbers of trees. When there are no tree roots, soil erodes and cannot absorb moisture. Without moisture, land becomes useless for farming.

Haiti has lost the greatest percentage of its forests of any country in this region. As a result of deforestation and its effects on soil, Haiti has trouble producing enough food to feed its people.

Loss of habitat has also caused a decline in wildlife diversity. Many valuable medicinal plants have been lost. Some Native American groups, such as the Miskito people in Honduras and Nicaragua, live in the rain forests along the Caribbean coast. For them, deforestation means losing their homes.

Reading Check What are the effects of deforestation?

When rain forests are destroyed, animals like the jaguar lose their homes and face extinction. ▶

Section 1 Assessment

Key Terms

1. What makes Panama an ideal place for building a canal?

2. How do tourists and tourism affect Central America and the Caribbean?

Key Ideas

3. Describe the effects of a hurricane on a country's land, structures, and people.

4. What is the relationship among climate, biodiversity, and tourism in Central America and the Caribbean?

5. How can large-scale farming harm the environment?

Think Critically

6. **Ask Questions** Referring to the graph that compares the number of year-round residents with foreign tourists, write a question for the Antigua and Barbuda minister of tourism.

7. **Draw Conclusions** Based on what you have learned about ecosystems and economic activities, what do you think might happen if one of the region's ecosystems was destroyed?

Essential Question

Is it better to be independent or interdependent?

8. How might the frequency of natural disasters affect a country's ability to be independent? Go to your Student Journal to record your answer.

GUIDE ON THE SIDE

Cause and Effect Have students read to determine the causes and effects of deforestation.

- What has led to widespread deforestation? (clearing of land for ranching and farming; demand for timber)

- What are the effects of deforestation? (soil erosion and reduction of farm land; loss of wildlife habitat and medicinal plants)

- In which country has deforestation caused widespread hunger? (Haiti)

- What effect would deforestation have on the Miskito people? (They would lose their home.)

SECTION 1 ASSESSMENT 1. narrow; between two oceans **2.** support economy, can cause environmental harm **3.** can harm people and cause destruction **4.** Climate supports biodiversity, which attracts tourists. **5.** can cause deforestation, harm coral reefs and marine life **6.** Sample: How does the large tourist population affect year-round residents? **7.** Sample: The loss of a regional ecosystem would negatively affect tourism. **8.** Sample: Damage caused by frequent natural disasters might cause reliance on other nations for economic assistance, limiting independence.

ANSWERS

History of Central America and the Caribbean

OBJECTIVES

Students will know

- characteristics of early civilizations in the region.
- colonizers relied on slavery and the export of the region's natural resources.

Students will be able to

- analyze causes and effects of colonization.
- decide if independence brought about great change or not.

SET EXPECTATIONS

In this section, students will

- read History of Central America and the Caribbean.
- categorize and debate the region's characteristics by time period.
- explore Caribbean colonial history online.

CORE CONCEPTS

You may wish to teach or reteach the following lessons from the Core Concepts Handbook:

- Trade, pp. 66–67
- Migration, pp. 78–79
- Political Systems, pp. 106–107

KEY

Differentiated Instruction

- **L1** Special Needs **L2** Extra Support
- **L3** On-Level **L4** Challenge

English Language Instruction

- **ELL** Beginner **ELL** Early Intermediate **ELL** Intermediate
- **ELL** Early Advanced **ELL** Advanced

1 Connect
Make learning meaningful

Make Connections Have students, in pairs, list every food they ate in the last week that contained sugar. Ask what they would do if they didn't have sugar. Ask, What other sweeteners come from products grown in the United States? (corn syrup, honey). As students read the section, have them think about how sugar shaped Middle American history.

L4 Challenge Have students make pamphlets about the dangers of sugar consumption.

Activate Prior Knowledge Remind students that in the previous section they learned about the region's physical geography and natural resources. Have them think about characteristics that might have led Europeans to establish colonies in Central America and the Caribbean.

ELL Early Advanced/Advanced Provide students with a two-column table, with "Motivation to Colonize" and "Physical Feature" as the two headings. Extend language by mapping the word *motivation* and related words such as *motive*.

Prepare Follow the steps in the section **Preview**. Preteach the Key Terms. Then have students complete *Word Wise* in their journals using in-text clues and the glossary for help.

2 Experience
Teach knowledge and skills

Read Use **Background** notes and **Guide on the Side** questions to model active reading. Have students use *Take Notes* in their journals to analyze causes and effects of colonization, independence, and foreign involvement in Central America and the Caribbean. Have students complete **21st Century Online Tutor** *Analyze Cause and Effect* and apply this skill to reading the section.

ELL Intermediate Have students use a chart to compare and contrast Mayan and early Caribbean societies.

L4 Challenge Have students read *Enrichment: Maya Math* to learn more about the academic achievements of the Maya.

Practice: myWorld Activity Students will move around the room to categorize descriptions of the region by historical time period. Students will then debate those categorizations. **Step-by-Step Instructions** and **More Activities** follow on the p. T44.

SECTION 2 RESOURCE GUIDE

FOR THE STUDENT

 worldgeography.com

- Culture Close-up
- Visual Glossary

Student Edition (print and online)
- History of Central America and the Caribbean

Student Journal (print and online)
- Section 2 Word Wise
- Section 2 Take Notes

21st Century Learning **Online Tutor**

- Analyze Cause and Effect
- Make Decisions

FOR THE TEACHER

my worldgeography.com **Teacher Center**
- Online Lesson Planner
- Presentations for Projection
- SuccessTracker

ProGuide: Middle America
- Lesson Plan, pp. T42–T43
- myWorld Activity Step-by-Step Instructions, p. T44
- Activity Support: Reflection, p. T45
- myWorld Geography Enrichment, p. T46
- Section Quiz, p. T47

Accelerating the Progress of ELLs
- Organizing Information Strategies, p. 48

---

3 Understand
Assess learning

Review Review students' work in their **Student Journals.**

Assess Knowledge and Skills Use the Section Assessment and Section Quiz to check students' progress.

Assess Understanding Review students' responses to the Section Assessment Essential Question prompt.

Remediate Use these strategies to review and remediate.

If students struggle to . . .	Try these strategies.
Analyze cause and effect	Have students make chain reaction diagrams for key events.
Sequence events	Assign additional practice with the **21st Century Online Tutor.**
Understand colonialism	Have students act out the flow of people and products between a colony and its home country.

ELL Support

ELL Objective Students will be able to use English to express cause-and-effect relationships.

Cultural Connections Have students use their native language to explain why people from their home country have migrated to the United States.

ELL Intermediate Content Tip Have students work in pairs to make a connection between the illustrations in the section and the definition of *encomienda*. Have them write cause-and-effect sentences about the *encomienda* system.

ELL Activity Assign a group of students to each part of Section 2. Tell them to create skits that summarize their part of the section and show how one event led to another.

myWorld Activity   **Step-by-Step Instructions**   25 min

Corners of History

OBJECTIVES

Students will

- categorize aspects of Middle American history by time period.
- analyze the effects of colonization and independence.

Activity Steps

1. Place signs in each corner of the room that read, Early Maya (A.D. 250–900), Colonialism (1492 to 1821), Early Independence (1821 to 1870), and Foreign Involvement (1870 to present).

2. Tell students that you will read one statement at a time meant to describe Central American and Caribbean society. Tell students to listen to the statement, and then move to the corner/time period that best suits the society described in the statement.

   L2 Extra Support Have students read the statements on the Activity Support before participating in the activity.

3. Then ask students to explain why they think the statement fits the time period. Ask students standing in different corners to defend their reasons for picking that time period.

LEARNING STYLE

- Kinesthetic
- Logical

21st Century Learning

- Make Decisions

MATERIALS

- Activity Support: Reflection, p. T45
- Signs for corners of room

4. After representatives from each corner have spoken, allow students to change corners if they have changed their minds. Repeat with remaining statements.

5. Discuss with the class why it is so hard to categorize these characteristics. Ask, How much did independence change Middle American society? How much did this society remain the same?

   ELL Intermediate/Early Advanced Have students break into groups and write down the characteristics of each time period on chart paper. Ask them to underline key words that define that time period.

6. Have students complete *Activity Support: Reflection* to summarize similarities and differences between each period of the region's history.

More Activities From myWorld Teachers

Local Connections Have students brainstorm examples of foreign businesses or products sold in their communities. Assign groups to make charts of pros and cons of foreign economic involvement (e.g., Saudi oil, Chilean fruit, and Japanese cars.)

Dictator for Hire Have students write a resume for a major Central American or Caribbean dictator from the 1900s (e.g., (Trujillo, Somoza, Batista). Resumes

should include jobs held before ruling the country as well as jobs held or places lived after losing power.)

 Maya Blockade Have students enact the theory that the stoppage of trade in the region led to the decline of the Maya. Set up a trading center with a symbolic stash of a trade item (for example, pencils can represent ears of corn), and have competing groups block "entries" into the center.

my worldgeography.com **Teacher Center** ➡ Find additional resources in the online Teacher Center.

Name _____ Class _____ Date _____

myWorld Activity Support   **Reflection**

Corners of History

Directions After participating with the class in Corners of History, summarize your experiences by writing the statements that fit with different time periods in their boxes. Statements will repeat. Then answer the reflection questions at the bottom of the page.

Statements
- The economy was based on agriculture and trade.
- Slavery was present.
- Few people owned land.
- Natural resources were protected.
- Foreign influence was strong.
- Local people controlled the wealth.

Early Maya (A.D. 250–900)	Colonialism (1492 to 1821)
Early independence (1821 to 1870)	Foreign involvement (1870 to present)

1. Which statements are true for only one period? Pick one and explain what you think makes this time period different from the others.

_____

_____

2. What changed with independence? What did not change?

_____

_____

Name _____ Class _____ Date _____

Enrichment: Maya Math

Directions Read the selection below. Then answer the questions and complete the activity.

The Maya writing system used three symbols to represent numbers. A shell represents 0, a dot is 1, and a horizontal bar is 5. Our system of counting uses place values based on factors of 10 (1's, 10's, 100's, and so on). The Maya system, however, used place values based on factors of 20 (1's, 20's, 400's, and so on). Maya place values went from top to bottom. In the example below that shows the number 754, the top value is determined by multiplying 400 by 1. The middle value is 20 $\times$ 17. The bottom value is 1 $\times$ 14. Adding the top (400), middle (340), and bottom (14) values results in 754.

Maya Numbers

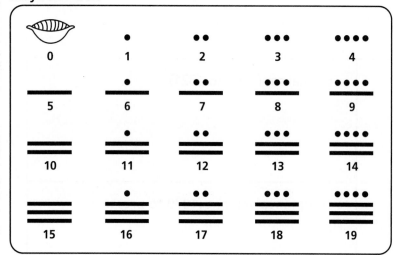

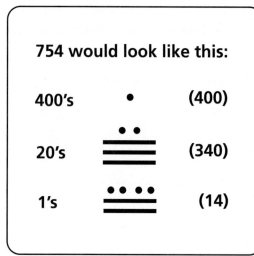

1. What symbols are used in the Maya system of numbers?

_____

2. Look at the example above that shows the number 754. How would you change the symbols to represent the number 755?

_____

Activity Working in teams, create at least two flash cards. Write a number on one side of the card. Then write the same number using Maya symbols on the other side. After completing the flash cards, exchange cards with another team. Play a game to see which team correctly "translates" the Maya numbers most quickly. For a second round, teams may subtract one Maya number from the other, writing the answer using Maya symbols.

Name _____ Class _____ Date _____

Section Quiz

Directions Answer the following questions using what you learned
in Section 2.

1. _____ The Maya
   a. lived in the Caribbean.
   b. developed a highly accurate calendar.
   c. had no organized religion.
   d. declined after Spanish colonization.

2. _____The Maya were organized into
   a. tribes.
   b. countries.
   c. colonies.
   d. city-states.

3. _____ What was the main purpose of the
   encomienda system?
   a. to provide Native Americans with land
   b. to establish sugar plantations
   c. to define the status of Native Americans
   d. to teach Christianity

4. _____ When Haiti won its independence, it
   a. gained the right of self-rule.
   b. gained additional land.
   c. was the last Caribbean country to gain
      independence.
   d. experienced an increase in slavery.

5. _____ Why did American investors gain
   economic influence in the Caribbean?
   a. The United States colonized the
      Caribbean islands.
   b. After independence, the region's
      economies depended on money from
      foreign investors.
   c. Fidel Castro sold Cuban industries to
      American companies.
   d. Caribbean businesses did not want to
      invest in the region's economies.

6. Complete the table below to show how foreign influence has
affected Central America and the Caribbean.

How did each of the following affect Central America and the Caribbean?
Encomienda system:
Slavery:
Foreign investment:

History of Central America and the Caribbean

- Model preparing to read by previewing the Key Ideas, Key Terms, headings, visuals, and captions. Have students make predictions about what they will learn. For ELL support, post the prompt, "I predict I will read about . . ."

- Preview and practice the reading skill, analyze cause and effect, by using examples from a popular book or movie plot.

- Teach this section's high-use Academic Vocabulary using the chart on the next page. Have students practice Academic Vocabulary and Key Terms by completing the *Word Wise* page in their journals.

Early Civilizations

- **Identify Details** Where did the early Maya settle? (in what is now Guatemala)

- **Identify Evidence** What evidence suggests that the Maya civilization was highly developed? (The Maya developed an accurate calendar and a writing system. They were organized into city-states and utilized irrigation.)

Mayan Writing Point out the image of Maya writing.

- Why do you think the writing was so hard to understand? (Sample: The meanings of the various symbols were not passed down to later generations.)

Reading Skill

Analyze Cause and Effect
While they read, have students practice this skill by completing the *Take Notes* graphic organizer in the **Student Journal.**

Section 2

History of Central America and the Caribbean

| Key Ideas | • Early civilizations in the region were organized agricultural and trading societies. | • European colonizers depended heavily upon slavery and exporting natural resources. | • While European colonies became independent nations, foreign powers remained influential. |

Key Terms • Maya • colony • encomienda • hacienda • independence • dictatorship

 Visual Glossary

Reading Skill: Analyze Cause and Effect Take notes using the graphic organizer in your journal.

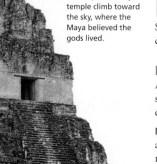

◀ The steps of a Maya temple climb toward the sky, where the Maya believed the gods lived.

Early civilizations in Central America and the Caribbean grew in the centuries before Europeans arrived. But when Spanish explorers began to seek gold in the 1500s, the conflict and colonization that followed changed the region forever.

Early Civilizations

Around 1000 B.C., Native Americans known as the **Maya** began settling in what is now Guatemala. Over time, the Maya culture developed into a great civilization and a center of trade.

Maya Civilization The Maya developed a highly accurate calendar and a system of writing that used symbols. They were skilled at mathematics, architecture, astronomy, weaving, and sculpture. Maya farmers grew maize, or corn, and other crops, often using irrigation.

The Maya were organized into city-states, each with its own ruler. Maya cities often fought each other for land and power, but trade helped unite Maya civilization. Each city had large pyramid-shaped temples. These temples

◀ Archaelogists and linguists have spent many years learning the complicated system of Mayan writing.

ACADEMIC VOCABULARY

High-Use Word	Definition and Sample Sentences
establish	*v.* to set up *Before beginning a new game, it is a good idea to establish the rules.*
import	*v.* to ship in from another country *Years ago, the United States began to import products made in China.*

were the sites of religious celebrations to honor the many Maya gods. Maya priests studied the stars and planets. Cities also had outdoor courts where Mayas played a special ball game.

Maya civilization began to decline around A.D. 900. Historians believe that this decline was caused by a combination of factors, including war, crop failures, and environmental problems.

Early Caribbean Peoples The Caribbean islands were home to two main groups of people now known as the Arawak and the Carib. They grew a variety of plants for food, gathered fruits, and harvested shellfish from the sea. Caribbean peoples used canoes for traveling among the islands. These islands were divided into villages and ruled by chiefs.

Reading Check Summarize the region's early civilizations.

Colonization and Slavery

In 1492, Christopher Columbus sailed across the Atlantic Ocean from Europe, arriving in the Bahamas. The Spanish explorers who followed him to the region established colonies and mined natural resources. In the process, they killed or enslaved millions of Native Americans.

Spanish Colonization Early Spanish explorers were in search of gold and other riches. They also wanted to convert the native people to Christianity. By the early 1500s, the Spanish had conquered the entire region and formed a colony in what is now Panama. A **colony** is a group of people living in a new territory with

ties to a distant state. The Spanish called this colony the Kingdom of Guatemala.

Leaders called viceroys ruled the Spanish colonies. The government <u>established</u> the encomienda (en koh mee EN dah) system. **Encomienda** was a legal system to control Native Americans in the Spanish colonies. Under encomienda, Spanish officials could tax Native Americans or force them to work. In return, Spaniards were required to teach them Christianity. But encomienda soon turned into a system of slavery without religious teaching. As a Spanish priest wrote,

> 66 [Spaniards] had as little concern for their souls as for their bodies, all the millions that have perished having gone to their deaths with no knowledge of God. 99
> —Bartolome de las Casas, 1542

establish, *v.,* to set up

Spaniards used violence to force Native Americans to work (top). Enslaved Africans later replaced Native Americans as laborers (bottom). ▼

 Culture Close-up

READING CHECK The Maya developed an advanced civilization in what is now Guatemala. In the Caribbean, the Arawak and the Carib grew and gathered food, lived in villages, and traveled between islands by canoe.

ANSWERS

- **Identify Details** Which main groups of people populated the Caribbean islands? (Arawak and Carib)
- **Cause and Effect** How did the early Caribbean people adapt to island living? (They built canoes for sea travel.)

Colonization and Slavery

- **Identify Details** What was the first colony established by Spanish explorers, and where was it located? (the Kingdom of Guatemala in what is now Panama)
- **Cause and Effect** How did the encomienda system affect Native Americans? (They were treated as slaves.)

➡ **Culture Close-up**

Have students visit myworldgeography.com to learn more about Caribbean colonial history

HISTORY

An Ill-Fated Union Formed in 1824, the United Provinces of Central America was a federal republic, its five states eventually becoming the nations of Guatemala, Honduras, El Salvador, Costa Rica, and Nicaragua. The Republic drew up a constitution that abolished slavery and named Guatemala City as its capital.

Unlike the United States, the United Provinces did not survive a civil war brought about by political dissensions. The republic lasted less than 20 years.

GUIDE ON THE SIDE

- **Cause and Effect** What led the Spanish to import African slaves? (the widespread death of Native Americans)

Ending Foreign Control

- **Sequence** Which nation was the first to shake off foreign control? (Haiti)

- **Identify Details** Who was Toussaint L'Ouverture? (He led the first rebellion in Haiti.)

- **Infer** What marked the end of Spanish rule in Central America? (The Kingdom of Guatemala declared itself free.)

Analyze Visuals Point out the Before and After chart.

- How did government change? (Monarchies were replaced by constitutional republics.)

- What changed about who held political power? (Former viceroys often became presidents.)

- How was land distribution similar or different after independence? (Land remained in the hands of a wealthy minority.)

myWorld Activity

Corners of History Find Step-by-Step Instructions and an Activity Support on pp. T44–T45. **(Kinesthetic/Logical)**

---

import, v., to ship in from another country

Spanish landowners created **haciendas,** or huge farms and ranches. Many native people had died from disease or abuse, so the Spanish <u>imported</u> enslaved Africans to work the land.

Slavery in the Caribbean By the 1600s, other European countries had formed Caribbean colonies. They grew cash crops, especially sugar cane, which required huge amounts of land and labor. As did the Spanish in Central America, these sugar planters imported enslaved Africans to do the work. Sugar, slaves, rum, tobacco, and molasses formed a triangular system of trade connecting the Caribbean, Europe, and Africa. This system of trade made the Europeans who ruled the colonies very wealthy.

myWorld Activity
Corners of History

Reading Check What was the encomienda system in the Spanish colonies?

Ending Foreign Control

For more than 200 years, European countries controlled the region. Unrest exploded in the 1800s.

Rebellion in Haiti In the late 1700s, the people of Saint-Domingue revolted against their French rulers. An enslaved man named Toussaint L'Ouverture (too SAN loo vehr TOOR) led the rebellion. In 1804, after years of fighting, the people declared their **independence,** or the right to rule themselves. They renamed the country Haiti.

Spanish Rule Ends In 1821, the Kingdom of Guatemala declared independence from Spain. Two years later, most of Central America formed the United Provinces of Central America. For years, the United Provinces struggled over political differences. By 1840, this state had broken into independent republics.

Before Independence

- Colonies are ruled by monarchies.
- Rulers live far away in Europe but tax people in the colonies.
- Colonial leaders called viceroys control large areas of land.
- Most native people and some enslaved Africans work the land that belongs to the viceroys.
- Almost everything grown or made in the colonies is exported to European markets.

Toussaint L'Ouverture was an inspiration to other colonists who wanted to break free from Europe. ▶

After Independence

- Independent constitutional republics are established.
- Former viceroys or landowners often become presidents of the new countries.
- Many poor landless people work for relatively few landowners.
- Republics are dependent on foreign markets to sell their goods.
- Exported goods benefit the landowners, making them richer.
- Landowners support dictators who keep matters the same.

READING CHECK The encomienda system let Spaniards rule over a piece of land and force Native Americans to work for them. At first, native people could pay a tax instead of working, but after a while this system became a form of slavery.

READING CHECK Castro seized property held by Americans in Cuba, causing the United States to break off relations with Cuba.

QUICK FACTS

The Panama Canal Construction of the Panama Canal began in 1904. Ten years later, the first ship traveled through the Canal's locks from the Atlantic to the Pacific. More than 50,000 laborers had worked on the project, which cost approximately $350 million to complete. Although vessels had been using the Canal for several years, the Canal did not formally open until 1920.

Depending on Outsiders After independence, many countries looked to foreign investors to help build their economies. Over time, the region's economies came to depend on other countries, especially the United States.

In the Caribbean, U.S. investors rebuilt and took control of industries such as sugar, coffee, and bananas. They also took over land and built enormous plantations. The United States government gained control of land in Panama and built the Panama Canal, an important trade link between the Atlantic and Pacific Oceans.

Dictatorship and Democracy While American economic influence grew, democracy did not. Throughout the 1900s, **dictatorships,** or governments controlled by a single leader, became common. Dictators like Fulgencio Batista of Cuba limited political freedom. However, Batista was able to develop Cuba's economy. As the Cuban economy grew, U.S. investors profited. Then Fidel Castro led a communist revolution in Cuba, taking power in 1959. When

Castro took U.S.-owned property, the United States ended relations with Cuba.

By the late 1900s, people in the region had grown tired of being controlled by dictators and other countries. Conflict broke out in many places. In Guatemala, a deadly civil war lasted nearly forty years. In Nicaragua in the 1970s, rebels took power from a dictatorship; in turn, a new dictatorship took power from the rebels. By the 1980s and 1990s, the last Caribbean colonies had finally gained their independence. Now they needed to make democracy work.

Reading Check What happened when Castro took power from Batista in Cuba?

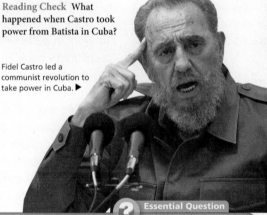

Fidel Castro led a communist revolution to take power in Cuba. ▶

- **Identify Evidence** How did the United States exert its influence in Panama? (by acquiring land and building the Panama Canal)
- **Summarize** In the 1900s what form of government was most common in the region? (dictatorship)
- **Cause and Effect** Why did the United States break off relations with Cuba? (Castro seized property owned by Americans.)

Section 2 Assessment

Key Terms
1. How did the encomienda system make Spain wealthy?
2. What makes a government a dictatorship?

Key Ideas
3. How did the Maya, the Carib, and the Arawak feed themselves?
4. Why did the Spanish begin to import enslaved Africans?
5. Why did newly independent nations look to foreign investors?

Think Critically
6. **Draw Conclusions** What do you think motivated Americans to invest in Central America and the Caribbean?
7. **Synthesize** What aspects of colonialism might have helped lead to dictatorships?

Essential Question
Is it better to be independent or interdependent?
8. Were the Spanish colonists independent or interdependent? Go to your Student Journal to record your answer.

SECTION 2 ASSESSMENT 1. The encomienda system provided free Native American labor. **2.** It has one leader with unlimited power. **3.** The Maya farmed; the Carib and Arawak farmed, gathered fruit, and harvested shellfish. **4.** The Spanish needed labor for large farms. **5.** They had little money and needed more to grow their economies. **6.** Americans probably believed that they could profit by investing in the region. **7.** The descendants of colonists were accustomed to having little political power. **8.** They were independent politically but dependent on Native American labor.

The Maya

OBJECTIVES

Students will

- describe characteristics of Maya culture.
- draw conclusions about the accomplishments of Maya civilization through its architecture and literature.
- **ELL** use *gruel*, *gourd* and other passage terms in original sentences.

SET EXPECTATIONS

In this primary source, students will

- read The Maya.
- develop a new way to learn and teach about Maya beliefs in the activity *Popul Vuh* for Kids.

1 Connect

Tell students to imagine that the remains of their school have been unearthed by archaeologists in A.D. 3000. Ask, What might the researchers think is evidence of the school's culture? Have students make a list of things they would and would not want to be interpreted as evidence of culture.

ELL **Intermediate** Point out that *civilization* shares the Latin root *civ-* (from *civilis*, meaning "citizen") with a number of other words common in social studies, including *civic* and *civil*. Prompt students to think of word families for the roots *liter* ("letters") and *fac/fact* ("do, make").

2 Learn

Preview Have students preview pictures and headings. Prompt them to try to draw comparisons between the various photographs and illustrations of Maya culture.

Read While students read The Maya, ask questions found in **Guide on the Side** to build understanding of the Key Idea and objectives.

ELL **Early Advanced** Point out to students how *gruel* and *gourd* are explained below the creation story. Ask students to find two other words in the passage for which they would like to know the exact meaning, such as *miracle* or *strength*. Tell them to use a dictionary to write definitions for the words and use each word in two different sentences.

myWorld Activity: *Popol Vuh* for Kids Announce that students are going to work in author-illustrator pairs to create a children's book around the Maya creation story. Tell pairs to use the story and the extra information on the handout to create a book that balances text and illustrations to respectfully explain the importance of corn in Maya culture to young children. Consider allowing students to visit lower-grade classrooms to read their books aloud. Have students use *Activity Support: Storyboards* to plan their book. **(Verbal/Visual)**

30 min

L4 **Challenge** Have partners write a review of their book. Remind them that the review should briefly summarize the book's subject matter, but then focus on how well the topic is covered and what young readers will enjoy.

3 Understand

Review Ask a group to role-play the Maya creation story. Have the rest of the class yell "Freeze!" every time the actors touch upon a key theme in the story, such as the power of the Maya gods. Discuss each pause.

Assess Have students write their responses to the Assessment questions in their notebooks. Then

read a list of adjectives and ask students which words describe what they know of the Maya.

Remediate If students struggle to understand the importance of the temple ruins, have them compare what they know about the ruins to a well-known, modern-day building, such as the White House. Discuss thematic similarities.

Name _____ Class _____ Date _____

myWorld Activity Support   Storyboards

Popol Vuh for Kids

Directions Reread the creation story from the *Popol Vuh.* Then read the additional facts about Maya culture below. Use all of this information to write and illustrate a children's book about the Maya creation story. Use the storyboards below to sketch and draft what you want each page to look like. Then create the book using separate sheets of paper.

- Corn was one of the most important crops the Maya grew. Having this reliable food source allowed the Maya to grow as a people and concentrate on things besides agriculture.

- The Maya worshipped a rain god, believing that this higher power provided the water that helped their corn grow.

- The maize, or corn, god was a symbol of Maya kings.

- The Maya believed that the four different colors of corn represented the four directions of Earth: north, south, east, and west.

Front Cover	Page 1	Page 2
Page 3	**Page 4**	**Page 5**
Page 6	**Page 7**	**Back Cover**

HISTORY

A Maya Treasure Although the *Popol Vuh* was not written until the mid-1500s, historians believe that it was probably part of the Maya oral tradition long before then. Many modern Maya consider the book, originally written in the native Guatemalan Quiché language, their equivalent of the Christian Bible, as the book contains everything from creation stories to the spiritual history of the Quiché. At the beginning of the 1700s, a Dominican priest in Guatemala succeeded in making a copy of the original manuscript. He also translated the book into Spanish. The original *Popol Vuh* was lost or destroyed sometime after that.

GUIDE ON THE SIDE

Draw Conclusions Help students discover parallel ideas in both sources. Use the introduction to highlight the ideas connecting developed civilizations with religion and architecture.

ANSWERS

Ⓐ a large stone pyramid with many steps

Ⓑ There were no motorized machines to help workers transport, lift, and place heavy stones.

Ⓒ This temple shows that Maya rulers were respected by the Maya people and powerful enough to order the construction of large temples.

Primary Source

The Maya

| Key Idea | • The Maya built great city-states in Central America, where they worshiped many gods. |

▲ A Maya sculpture

Maya civilization reached its height around A.D. 250. Religion was an important element of Maya civilization. Maya city-states included great pyramid-shaped temples where the Maya worshiped their gods. The Temple of the Inscriptions, in what is now Palenque, Mexico, was built as the tomb of a Maya ruler. The *Popol Vuh* is a written description of the Maya religion and gods. This book was written in the 1500s, after the Spanish conquered the region. It explains the Maya belief that the gods made people from corn, the most important Maya crop.

Examine the photograph on the right. Then answer the questions below.

Ⓐ **Identify Details** Describe the appearance of this temple.

Ⓑ **Analyze Primary Sources** Why would this temple have been hard to build?

Ⓒ **Infer** What does this temple suggest about the power of Maya rulers?

A Maya Temple

Temple of the Inscriptions, Palenque ▶

ANALYZE THE DOCUMENTS

1. Sample: The Maya may have believed that their kings were chosen by the gods, since they had such special responsibilities and power. Kings probably enforced certain religious beliefs and practices.

2. Sample: The high level of development seen in Maya city-states and religious beliefs indicates that the Maya had established a society that included traditions and practices. Buildings were carefully planned and constructed within cities that were

21st Century Learning   DRAW CONCLUSIONS

To help students draw conclusions about the themes and concepts linking the Temple of Inscriptions with the creation story from the *Popol Vuh,* prompt them to think about the importance of architecture (especially memorials) and religion in modern-day society. Remind them that while the ideas of elaborate tombs and men made from corn may seem unusual to us today, many of our own practices and beliefs, in our own highly developed civilization, stem from similarly crafted concepts. Work with students to create a backward diagram showing how architecture and religious belief systems connect to advanced civilizations. For example, students may link religious beliefs backward a step to a people's need for explanations, then backward another step to people's questions about life and death.

Read the text on the right. Stop at each circled letter. Then answer the question with the same letter on the left.

D Identify Main Ideas and Details According to this account, who discovered corn?

E Infer Who are the gods in this passage? How do you know?

F Draw Conclusions Why might the Maya have believed that the first people were made from corn?

gruel, *n.,* thin, watery cereal
gourd, *n.,* dried, hollow shell of a squash

Popol Vuh

66 We will now return to the story of man's creation. . . . The corn used to create the first men was found in the place called Paxil and K'ayala'. Yak the wildcat, Utiw the coyote, K'el the parrot and Joj the crow, were the creatures who **D** discovered this food. . . .

Then our Makers Tepew and **E** Q'uk'umatz began discussing the creation of our first mother and father. Their flesh was made of white and yellow corn. . . . Then Grandmother Ixmukane ground the white and yellow ears of corn to make enough <u>gruel</u> to fill nine <u>gourds</u> to provide strength, muscle and power to the four new men.

The names of the first four men were, in order, B'alam Ki'tze', B'alam Aq'ab', Majukutaj **F** and Iq' B'alam. Only a miracle could have made the first fathers out of . . . corn. **99**

—*Popol Vuh: A Sacred Book of the Maya,*
retold by Victor Montejo, translated by David Unger

A Maya codex, or folding book ▼

ANSWERS

D Yak the wildcat, Utiw the coyote, K'el the parrot, and Joj the crow

E Tepew, Q'uk'umatz, and Ixmukane; I can tell they are gods because they have proper names and titles like "Makers" and "Grandmother." They are also described as doing things humans could not do.

F Sample: Since corn was the most important Maya crop, it makes sense that the Maya would believe that people were created from this strength-giving plant.

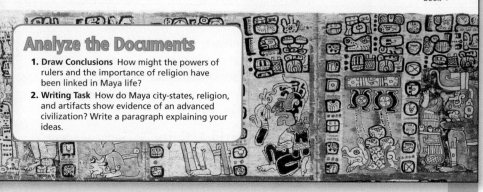

Analyze the Documents

1. **Draw Conclusions** How might the powers of rulers and the importance of religion have been linked in Maya life?
2. **Writing Task** How do Maya city-states, religion, and artifacts show evidence of an advanced civilization? Write a paragraph explaining your ideas.

---

also carefully planned. Architecture reflected people's views of rulers and their eternal place in society. The Maya religion connected the creation of man with a life-giving crop, showing that the Maya had thought about the cause-and-effect relationship between humans, gods, and everyday life. The fact that Maya religious beliefs were recorded in writing proves that the Maya were concerned about preserving and passing on their beliefs.

Central America and the Caribbean Today

OBJECTIVES

Students will know

- the cultural influences of African, European, and indigenous groups.
- the political and economic challenges to the region.

Students will be able to

- summarize effects of foreign influence.
- compare viewpoints on free trade.

SET EXPECTATIONS

In this section, students will

- read Central America and the Caribbean Today.
- analyze different perspectives on DR-CAFTA.
- learn Spanish phrases online.

CORE CONCEPTS

You may wish to teach or reteach the following lessons from the Core Concepts Handbook:

- Economic Development, pp. 64–65
- Trade, pp. 66–67
- Cultural Diffusion and Change, pp. 96–97

KEY

Differentiated Instruction

L1 Special Needs **L2** Extra Support
L3 On-Level **L4** Challenge

English Language Instruction

ELL Beginner **ELL** Early Intermediate **ELL** Intermediate
ELL Early Advanced **ELL** Advanced

---

1 Connect
Make learning meaningful

Make Connections Ask students to think about their own cultural practices (holidays, music, clothing, food, religion, etc.) and describe something they do that comes from a mixture of different cultures (examples: eating a Vietnamese sandwich on French bread or listening to a song that samples American hip-hop and Indian pop music).

ELL **Intermediate** Have students identify a way in which their family's culture combines American traditions with traditions from their home country.

Activate Prior Knowledge Remind students that in the previous section they learned about colonization by European powers. Ask them to predict how colonization might affect life in the region today.

L1 **Special Needs** Have students look at the pictures of the people from different backgrounds in this section. Ask them to explain what makes their backgrounds different.

Prepare Follow the steps in the section **Preview**. Preteach the Key Terms. Then have students complete *Word Wise* in their journals using in-text clues and the glossary for help.

2 Experience
Teach knowledge and skills

Read Use **Background Notes** and **Guide on the Side** questions to model active reading. Have students use *Take Notes* to summarize the history of the region. Have students complete the Summarize Lesson on the **21st Century Online Tutor**, and apply what they learn to reading the section.

L4 **Challenge** Assign small groups to summarize the section in as few words as possible. Have one student start, then another student pick up where that student left off, and continue until the whole section content is covered.

ELL **Intermediate/Early Advanced** While students read about political challenges, have students name major problems people face in the region (poverty, disease, unemployment) and make word maps with a translation for each word.

 Practice: myWorld Activity Students will read two quotes from opposing sides of the debate on free trade in the region and compare the different viewpoints. **Step-by-Step Instructions** and **More Activities** follow on p. T52.

SECTION 3 RESOURCE GUIDE

FOR THE STUDENT

my worldgeography.com Student Center
- Data Discovery
- Language Lesson

Student Edition (print and online)
- Central American and the Caribbean Today

Student Journal (print and online)
- Section 3 Word Wise
- Section 3 Take Notes

21st Century Learning Online Tutor
- Summarize
- Compare Viewpoints

FOR THE TEACHER

my worldgeography.com Teacher Center
- Online Lesson Planner
- Presentations for Projection
- SuccessTracker

ProGuide: Middle America
- Section 3 Lesson Plan, pp. T50–T51
- myWorld Activity Step-by-Step Instructions, p. T52
- Activity Support: Viewpoints, p. T53
- myWorld Geography Enrichment, p. T54
- Section Quiz, p. T55

Accelerating the Progress of ELLs
- Peer Learning Strategies, p. 46

---

3 Understand
Assess learning

Review Review students' work in their **Student Journals.**

Assess Knowledge and Skills Use the Section Assessment and Section Quiz to check students' progress.

Assess Understanding Review students' responses to the Section Assessment Essential Question prompt.

Remediate Use these strategies to review and remediate.

If students struggle to . . .	Try these strategies.
Understand the causes of a diaspora	As a class, brainstorm reasons for leaving one's homeland.
Compare viewpoints	Assign additional practice with the **21st Century Online Tutor.**
Understand free trade	Ask students to come up with reasons for placing taxes on foreign products.

ELL Support

ELL Objective Students will identify categories of culture in English.

Cultural Connections To connect students to Luis's experience of working to help his family and to pay for his education, let students use their native language to describe similarities and differences between their own lives and that of Luis.

ELL Early Advanced Content Tip Point out the term *DR-CAFTA* and explain each word represented by the acronym. Then ask why a hyphen might be used to connect Dominican Republic to Central America.

ELL Activity Make and distribute index cards, each with a category such as music, sports, food, religion, or other tradition. Have students find examples of the category in the section and write the word(s) on the card. Allow students time to read through the section to find answers. **(Visual/Linguistic)**

myWorld Activity   **Step-by-Step Instructions**

 30 min

Is Free Fair?

OBJECTIVES
Students will
- compare points of view for and against DR-CAFTA.
- identify the effects of free trade agreements on weak economies.

LEARNING STYLE
- Verbal
- Logical

21st Century Learning
- Compare Viewpoints

MATERIALS
- Activity Support: Viewpoints, p. T53

Activity Steps

1. Post the major aspects of DR-CAFTA and review with students.

2. Have students work in groups of three to read quotes from supporters and opponents of DR-CAFTA. Students should read quotes at least twice.

ELL **Beginner/Early Intermediate** Let students act out free trade and protected trade using manipulatives. Post product prices for students to see the difference.

3. Have students answer the analysis questions on the Activity Support and complete the chart listing reasons to support and reasons to oppose the free trade agreement. Students should use information from the chapter in addition to the quotes.

L2 **Extra Support** Help students to define the terms *supporter* and *opponent*. Explain that *support* is a synonym for *help* and *oppose* is a synonym for *fight*.

4. In these small groups, have students brainstorm recommendations to amend DR-CAFTA. Have students consider these questions:

- If a change to DR-CAFTA means big countries would profit less, how would you justify that to them?
- Can small countries get ahead without free trade? Why or why not?

5. Have students share their recommendations or compromises with the class.

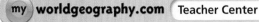
More Activities From myWorld Teachers

Local Connections Have students select a local cultural tradition and make diagrams showing its multiple ethnic influences (e.g., combining early American traditions and those of a more recent immigrant group). **(Visual)**

What's in a Song? Play a sample of Caribbean music (e.g., salsa, calypso) and ask students to identify the influences on the song—language,

instruments, etc. Ask students to describe what the song might say about its culture. **(Rhythmic)**

 Head of State Have students make a board game in which they are rulers of Central American or Caribbean nations. Each ruler has a budget. As they proceed, they face challenges such as natural disasters and decide how to use their money. **(Logical)**

my **worldgeography.com** (**Teacher Center** ➔) Find additional resources in the online Teacher Center.

Name _____ Class _____ Date _____

myWorld Activity Support   **Viewpoints**

Is Free Fair?

Directions Read the following quotes about the Dominican Republic-Central America Free Trade Agreement (DR-CAFTA), also known as CAFTA. Answer the questions and fill in the table.

Quotes on DR-CAFTA

1. "There is a line of businesses waiting for the starting gun, and now they have it with CAFTA . . . I have in my hands various letters from Brazilian, Korean, and U.S. companies who have wanted to invest here, but only on the condition that CAFTA passed."

> —Henry Fransen, in "Central American Leaders Praise Passage of CAFTA," *Los Angeles Times,* July 7, 2005

Based on Mr. Fransen's statement, what do you think will be one result of DR-CAFTA?

_____

_____

2. "Where is the evidence that [CAFTA] is going to develop us? . . . This is going to create more poverty . . . I never imagined CAFTA was going to be so one sided. The law of the jungle benefits the big beast. We are a very small beast."

> —Ottón Solís, in "U.S. Trade Pact Divides the Central Americans," *New York Times,* August 21, 2005

What do you think Mr. Solís meant to say about CAFTA by the underlined sentence? Who does he think will benefit? Who will not?

_____

_____

Reasons to Oppose CAFTA	**Reasons to Support CAFTA**

Name _____ Class _____ Date _____

Enrichment: Microcredit—Helping to Reduce Poverty

Directions Read the selection below. Answer the questions that follow.

The Grameen foundation makes tiny loans to help the world's poor start their own businesses. The foundation works with other organizations that operate in various regions around the world. One of these organizations—Esperanza, International—grants microloans to people in the Dominican Republic.

Dieula is a woman living in the Dominican Republic. To support herself and her two children, she began selling snacks to people in her neighborhood. However, she had almost no capital, or available money, to invest in her business and help it grow. Then she received a loan from Esperanza of 2,000 pesos, or 68 dollars.

Dieula paid off her loan in 6 months at 2 percent interest, with a payment every two weeks. She also increased her capital to 2,500 pesos. She began earning 40 to 50 pesos every day. Dieula received a second loan of 3,000 pesos, or 102 dollars, to help expand her business even more.

Esperanza Loan Program	
Loans granted	81,462
Businesses created	39,931
Repayment rate	97.68%
Current clients	18,466
Average loan	6,640.92 pesos
Borrowers	87.4% women

Source: Esperanza, International, Inc., July 1, 2009

1. Why was Dieula eligible for the loan program?

_____

_____

2. Do you think the Esperanza loan program is successful? Explain.

_____

_____

Name _____ Class _____ Date _____

Section Quiz

Directions Answer the following questions using what you learned
in Section 3.

1. _____ What is Santeria?
   a. the official religion of Guatemala
   b. a language spoken on the coast of
      Honduras
   c. a combination of Catholic and West
      African beliefs
   d. a religion that worships Iwa

2. _____ Carnival is
   a. a traditional Mayan festival.
   b. rarely celebrated in the Caribbean.
   c. a popular Cuban religion.
   d. a blend of different religious traditions.

3. _____ Millions of people have joined the
   diaspora because they
   a. dislike the region's climate.
   b. want to learn another language.
   c. hope to escape poverty.
   d. are bored.

4. _____ The main purpose of DR-CAFTA is to
   encourage
   a. free trade.
   b. large-scale farming.
   c. foreign investment.
   d. tourism.

5. _____ Which of the following statements
   is true?
   a. Microcredit is a way for tourists to pay
      for trips to the region.
   b. Microcredit and ecotourism have helped
      strengthen regional economies.
   c. Ecotourism has helped strengthen
      economies, but microcredit has not.
   d. Farmers are the least likely to benefit
      from microcredit.

6. In the appropriate section of the table, enter one positive and one
   negative effect of <u>free trade</u> on each group listed.

Positive Effect	Group	Negative Effect
	Farmers	
	Factory workers	
	Foreign investors	

Central American and the Caribbean Today

- Model preparing to read by previewing the Key Ideas, Key Terms, headings, visuals, and captions. Have students make predictions about what they will learn. For ELL support, post the prompt, "I predict I will read about . . . "

- Preview and practice the reading skill, summarize, by using examples from your community.

- Teach this section's high-use Academic Vocabulary using the chart on the next page. Have students practice Academic Vocabulary and Key Terms by completing the *Word Wise* page in their journals.

GUIDE ON THE SIDE

Woven Cultures

- **Identify Details** What is the ethnic background of most people in the Caribbean? (African)

- **Identify Details** What religion do most people in the Caribbean practice? (Catholicism)

- What elements make up the region's cultural diversity? (different religions and languages)

Reading Skill

Summarize While they read, have students practice this skill by completing the *Take Notes* graphic organizer in the **Student Journal.**

Section 3

Central America and the Caribbean Today

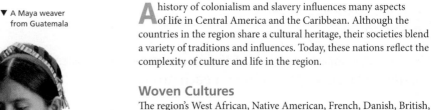

| Key Ideas | • Africans, Europeans, and indigenous people have all influenced Caribbean and Central American culture. | • Many Central American and Caribbean countries have democratic governments that change frequently. | • Free trade and ecotourism are having important effects on the region's economy. |

| Key Terms | • carnival • ecotourism | • Santeria | • diaspora | • microcredit | | Visual Glossary |

Reading Skill: Summarize Take notes using the graphic organizer in your journal.

▼ A Maya weaver from Guatemala

A history of colonialism and slavery influences many aspects of life in Central America and the Caribbean. Although the countries in the region share a cultural heritage, their societies blend a variety of traditions and influences. Today, these nations reflect the complexity of culture and life in the region.

Woven Cultures

The region's West African, Native American, French, Danish, British, and Spanish cultures weave together to form a diverse society. Most people in the Caribbean are of African descent and many people in the region speak Spanish, but there is great diversity in religion, ethnicity, language, and other aspects of culture.

Religion in the Caribbean Today, 90 percent of the people in the Caribbean are Roman Catholic. Still, the Caribbean's cultural celebrations, such as carnival, mix African, Native American, and European religious traditions. **Carnival** is a religious festival in late winter primarily observed by Roman Catholics. In the Caribbean, carnival includes large parades with bright costumes, music, and dancing that show the influence of West African culture. Most Caribbean countries celebrate carnival.

ACADEMIC VOCABULARY

High-Use Word	Definition and Sample Sentence
restrict	*v.* to limit or prevent *The contest rules restrict professionals from entering.*
luxury	*n.* pleasure or comfort *The Olympic-sized swimming pool was a luxury.*

Closer Look

One Region, Many Faces

Most people in Central America and the Caribbean have been influenced by a number of different cultures. The religions people practice, the art they make, and the languages they speak show how the region's people have created new cultures from many traditions.

THINK CRITICALLY **How do different cultures affect the region?**

▲ Caribbean music is known for its percussion, a tradition strongly influenced by West African music.

Haiti's official languages are French and Creole, a version of French influenced by African languages.

Native American languages are common in Guatemala. This boy speaks the Mayan language Achi.

This girl from Puerto Rico speaks Spanish and English, but she has Native American ancestors.

Like most other people from the Dominican Republic, Luis speaks Spanish.

Language Lesson

In Cuba, a popular religion called **Santeria** combines Catholic and West African beliefs. For example, the Santeria god Changó is a spirit from an ancient African religion. In Haiti, voodoo also includes elements of Catholic and West African beliefs. In Jamaica, Rastafarianism combines Christianity with the belief that the former emperor of Ethiopia descended from Israel's King Solomon and was divine. Trinidad has a growing number of believers in Hinduism and Islam. Recently, some Central American and Caribbean people have joined Protestant churches.

Indigenous Traditions Mestizos, or people of Spanish and indigenous background, are the largest ethnic group in Central America. In Guatemala, however, the Maya are the largest ethnic group. Most Guatemalans speak a form of Quechua (KECH wuh) as their first language, although they learn Spanish in school. Many Mayas mix traditional religious rituals with European ones, such as combining the names of Catholic saints with stories about Maya gods. Most Maya women wear traditional, multicolored woven fabrics.

THINK CRITICALLY Different cultures lead to a diversity of religion, language, and art in the region.

Closer Look

One Region, Many Faces

- **Compare and Contrast** What common language do the young people from the Dominican Republic and Puerto Rico share? (Spanish)

- **Synthesize** How do the four young people reflect cultural diversity? (They speak a variety of languages.)

 Language Lesson

Have students go to myworldgeography.com, where Luis will teach them to say "Hello," "Thank you," and more in his native language, Spanish.

Western Hemisphere   **259**
World Geography   **239**

GOVERNMENT

Plagued by Instability Although Haiti was the first Caribbean colony to achieve independence, the Republic of Haiti has been extremely unstable. The country's constitution, approved in 1987, was almost immediately suspended. Since then, Haiti has vacillated between military government and constitutional rule.

GUIDE ON THE SIDE

- **Infer** How do immigrants contribute to the economies of their homelands? (by sending money home to their families)

- **Synthesize** How has the region's diaspora led to cultural diffusion? (Traditions of the immigrants have blended with those of the countries in which they settle.)

Government and Change

- **Identify Details** Which country has the most stable democracy in the region? (Costa Rica)

- **Summarize** Why do governments in the region tend to be unstable? (Widespread political corruption and social unrest weaken them.)

> **Data Discovery**

- Have students visit myworldgeography.com to see more data about life in the region.

Going Global Many people in Central America and the Caribbean face widespread poverty. As a result, some people have migrated to North America or Europe in search of work. This spread of people from one place to many others is called a **diaspora**. After finding jobs, many immigrants send money, or remittances, to support their families.

Wherever people go, they bring their food, music, and beliefs. This leads to cultural diffusion, or the spread of cultural traits. Regional foods such as burritos and Cuban sandwiches are now popular in North America, Europe, and parts of Asia. Caribbean music has also traveled far from its roots. Salsa from Puerto Rico, merengue from the Dominican Republic, and reggae from Jamaica can be heard in many parts of the world.

Reading Check In what ways is Caribbean culture a blend of other cultures?

Government and Change

Central American and Caribbean people live in a region of change. People migrate to other countries and then return. Hurricanes can destroy crops and homes. Even governments can change quickly.

Democracy in the Region Most governments in Central America are presidential democracies in which a president is the head of government. In the Caribbean, many countries are democracies with parliamentary systems. In a parliamentary system, a prime minister is chosen from the parliament, or the legislative body of government. Most countries in the region select leaders in democratic elections. Often, citizens are legally required to vote.

Costa Rica has the region's most stable democracy. Costa Ricans have been electing their rulers since 1899. However, most of the region's democracies are less stable. Governments in poorer countries may change if voters are unhappy that leaders have failed to improve living conditions.

In fact, the lack of social services such as healthcare and education can lead to widespread anger and violence. Military takeovers and political violence are common. In Guatemala, civil war made

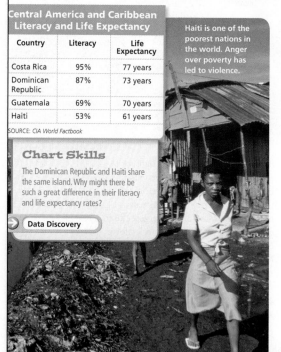

Central America and Caribbean Literacy and Life Expectancy		
Country	Literacy	Life Expectancy
Costa Rica	95%	77 years
Dominican Republic	87%	73 years
Guatemala	69%	70 years
Haiti	53%	61 years

SOURCE: *CIA World Factbook*

Haiti is one of the poorest nations in the world. Anger over poverty has led to violence.

Chart Skills

The Dominican Republic and Haiti share the same island. Why might there be such a great difference in their literacy and life expectancy rates?

> **Data Discovery**

ANSWERS

CHART SKILLS Haiti may have fewer resources from which to create jobs and fund education.

READING CHECK The Caribbean blends many languages, diverse ethnic backgrounds, and a variety of cultural traditions.

HISTORY

A Matter of Record The Guatemalan Civil War raged from 1960 to 1996. During that time 200,000 people were killed, while tens of thousands simply disappeared without a trace. At the time of the 1996 Peace Accord, police officials denied the existence of records documenting police action during the conflict.

In July 2005, however, tens of millions of these very documents were discovered in a decaying building near Guatemala City. Since then, archive investigators have been working to preserve and organize the records. It is believed that information in the documents may help convict those accused of human rights abuses, as well as shed light on the fate of the many "disappeared," or people who were killed but whose deaths were never made public.

democracy almost impossible until a 1996 peace agreement. In Haiti, 20,000 U.S. troops occupied the country to end a violent uprising in 1994. Since 2004, thousands of United Nations troops have helped keep peace in Haiti.

Dictatorship in Cuba Although most countries have removed their dictators, Cuba has not. Fidel Castro was the dictator of Cuba from 1959 to 2008, when he designated his brother Raúl to replace him. Cuba is a socialist republic with a command economy. The Communist Party is the only official political party.

Cubans cannot choose their leader, but they do vote for representatives to the National Assembly. These elections are unfair, however, since most races have only a single candidate. While Cuba restricts political and economic freedom, the government offers some social services that neighboring countries lack. For example, college and healthcare are practically free for Cubans.

Calls for Change Movements to improve the lives of people in the Caribbean and Central America continue. Throughout the region, there is a call to improve education and healthcare. In some places, voters have elected leaders who believe that government must help the poor and have more control over the economy. In other countries, such as the Dominican Republic, voters have turned to conservative leaders with the hope that they will be tough on crime and encourage foreign investments.

Reading Check What makes it difficult to achieve a stable democracy?

Freeing Up the Economy

One of the region's major economic goals is to increase capital investment, or investment in factories and technology. Capital investment can lead to economic growth. Government leaders often encourage foreign companies to build factories and other facilities in their countries. Countries also seek to improve human capital through education and training for workers.

Free-Trade Agreements One way the region's countries work to improve their economies is through free-trade agreements. Free trade is a system in which goods and services are traded between countries without government restrictions such as tariffs. Members of a free-trade association work to increase the amount of goods traded and to reduce taxes on products made in one member country and sold in another.

restrict, v., to limit or prevent

Costa Rica has a stable government, a stable economy, and a relatively high standard of living.

- **Compare and Contrast** How is Cuba's government different from those of most other countries in the region? (Cuba is still a dictatorship.)
- **Summarize** How have recent elections indicated a demand for change? (through the election of leaders who believe in providing social services or who will be tough on crime)

Freeing Up the Economy

- **Identify Main Ideas** Why do many countries in the region encourage foreign investment? (to improve their economies.)
- **Cause and Effect** Why do countries enter into free trade agreements? (to reduce taxes on goods traded and increase trade among participating nations)

Analyze Visuals Point out the image of a Costa Rican market.

- How does the image reflect the country's standard of living? (There is a variety of produce for sale. People are well dressed.)

READING CHECK Corruption and military takeovers make it difficult to maintain a stable democracy. Also, people need better schools, pay, and healthcare, and these unmet needs can lead to attempts to overthrow the government. Natural disasters can also make people unhappy and cause political instability.

ANSWERS

ECONOMICS

It's Only Fair Many small farmers have begun to benefit from fair trade. Fair Trade certification benefits farmers in 58 countries, including many in Central America and the Caribbean. Products such as coffee and bananas that bear the Fair Trade label assure consumers that the farmer will receive a fair price, even if the world market shifts, and that the product has been sustainably raised.

Workers on Fair Trade-certified farms have safer working conditions as well as living wages, meaning they are likely to be able to afford their basic needs with the money they are paid.

GUIDE ON THE SIDE

- **Synthesize** Who is most likely to benefit from free trade? (wealthy countries)

- **Draw Conclusions** How is land reform helping small farmers make a profit? (It enables farmers to own their land.)

- **Summarize** Why might a farming cooperative be more successful than an individual small farm? (Farmers work together and share profits.)

Chart Skills Have students look at the data shown in the chart.

- In what year did market and fair trade prices reach the same level? (2008)

myWorld Activity

Is Free Fair? Find Step-by-Step Instructions and an Activity Support on pp. T52–T53. **(Verbal/Logical)**

Data Discovery

- Have students visit myworldgeography.com to learn more about the economy of Central America and the Caribbean.

Market Price versus Fair-Trade Price of Coffee

Price per pound / Year

SOURCE: International Coffee Organization and Equal Exchange ■ Market ■ Fair Trade

Chart Skills

Fair trade can help guarantee stable prices and wages, while market prices can go up and down quickly. How does the market price for coffee compare to the fair-trade price?

Data Discovery

myWorldActivity
Is Free Fair?

One example of a free-trade association is the Caribbean Community (Caricom). Another is the Central America-Dominican Republic-United States Free Trade Association (CAFTA-DR), which also includes the United States.

Benefits and Drawbacks There are benefits and drawbacks to international free-trade agreements. Low taxes can encourage foreign businesses to build factories, creating jobs. CAFTA-DR has helped increase manufacturing in the region. However, some people worry that free trade helps wealthy countries more than poor countries. For these people, fair trade offers more benefits. Supporters of fair trade believe in paying workers fair wages and protecting the environment. They are often willing to pay more for goods that have been produced fairly.

Reforming Farms Free trade also affects farming. Farmers produce large amounts of food for free markets, and they often use a great deal of pesticides and fertilizer. This can harm the environment. In addition, most farmers do not own the crops they raise and thus cannot profit from international trade.

A few countries, such as Guatemala, have passed land-reform laws. These laws take some land from powerful landowners and divide it among poor farmers. Poor farmers can sometimes get small loans, called **microcredit,** to start their own farms. Some farmers form cooperatives, or groups of people who share the profits of their business. Many coffee and cacao growers now belong to cooperatives.

Reading Check **How are people trying to improve the region's economy?**

CORE CONCEPTS: PEOPLE'S IMPACT ON THE ENVIRONMENT

Review Core Concepts 4.3 to refocus students' attention on the ways in which humans negatively impact the natural environment. Discuss these factors within the context of tourism. Then discuss ways in which an ecological approach to tourism can minimize, or possibly even reverse, environmental damage to tourism destinations.

Ecotourism

Large <u>luxury</u> tourist resorts can cause environmental problems by using large amounts of resources, such as clean water. Still, tourism is an important part of the region's economy. One growing type of tourism is **ecotourism,** or tourism that focuses on the environment and seeks to minimize environmental impact. Ecotourism often involves exploring nature on foot or horseback. Tourists may sleep in simple huts or cabins. They may eat local food and require fewer imported goods to meet their needs.

Some people worry that ecotourism will change native cultures or harm natural habitats. But the Kuna Yala Reserve in Panama provides a successful example of ecotourism. In this case, the indigenous people themselves plan and manage an ecotourism program.

❝ [The Kuna Yala recognize] the importance of their natural surroundings and the need to protect their culture … [They know] how to manage the growth of tourism. ❞
—a Costa Rican travel agent

luxury, *n.,* pleasure or comfort

Reading Check What are the benefits of ecotourism?

my Story 📷 **Photo**

Luis's job as a tour guide depends on ecotourism.

Ecotourism

- **Cause and Effect** What is one environmental impact of large tourism facilities? (overuse of resources such as water)

- **Compare and Contrast** How does ecotourism differ from tourism in general? (Ecotourism focuses on the environment.)

- **Analyze Text** Why might the involvement of indigenous peoples strengthen ecotourism? (They are familiar with their countries' natural environments.)

Section 3 Assessment

Essential Question

❓ Is it better to be independent or interdependent?

Key Terms

1. What are some effects of the Caribbean diaspora?

2. How has ecotourism affected Central America and the Caribbean?

Key Ideas

3. Describe the cultures in Central America and the Caribbean.

4. What causes democratic governments in the region to change frequently?

5. How might land reform, microcredit, and cooperatives affect the economy?

Think Critically

6. **Compare and Contrast** How are the governments of Cuba and Costa Rica different?

7. **Compare Viewpoints** How might a small farmer's and an American factory owner's viewpoints on CAFTA-DR differ?

8. In what ways are the economies of Central America and the Caribbean independent and interdependent? Go to your Student Journal to record your answer.

SECTION 3 ASSESSMENT 1. reduced populations, stronger economies, cultural diffusion **2.** by boosting economies and helping to preserve natural environments **3.** a blend of African, European, and indigenous cultures **4.** political instability, poverty **5.** They strengthen the economy by supporting local enterprises. **6.** Cuba is a dictatorship; Costa Rica is a democratic republic. **7.** small farmer: negative, because of increased competition; American factory owner: positive, because DR-CAFTA increases trade **8.** Independent: government efforts to increase investment, improve human capital; interdependent: foreign investment, trade agreements

Cuba: Revolution to Today

OBJECTIVES
Students will

- learn about the political, economic, and social changes that have taken place in Cuba over the past several decades.
- express opinions about what changes should be made to improve conditions within Cuba.
- **ELL** determine when and how to change tenses.

SET EXPECTATIONS
In this case study, students will

- read Cuba: Revolution to Today.
- act as international observers in Cuba and compile a report in the activity *Report on Cuba*.

---

1 Connect

Ask students to describe major changes that have taken place in their lives and identify which had negative consequences. Have them free-write on the following questions: *When a change made things worse, how long did it take you to realize that another change was needed to make things better? Why do you think this sometimes happens?*

ELL **Early Intermediate** Provide scaffolding for switching between the past and present tenses: *When [the change] took place, I _____ . But now I _____ .* Repeat with verbs like *felt/feel* and *was/is* and "clue" phrases like *back then* and *at present*.

---

2 Learn

Preview Have students preview graphics and headings. Ask them to try shifting their frame of reference now and then as they read to consider the information in the text from different points of view.

Read While students read Cuba: Revolution to Today, ask questions found in **Guide on the Side** to build understanding of Key Ideas and objectives.

L2 Extra Support Ask partners to create and add to a Cuba timeline as they read.

L4 Challenge After making a timeline, have students label the "changemaker" in each interval (for example, for the event "1902–1950s," the changemaker would be the United States). Have partners discuss the effects of the different changemakers.

myWorld Activity: Report on Cuba
Tell partners that they are acting as international observers from the United Nations Development Programme (UNDP), an organization that tries to help people in developing countries improve their lives. They will investigate the economy, social conditions, and the overall standard of living among Cubans. They will then make recommendations for steps the UNDP should take to improve life in Cuba. Later, discuss common suggestions. Have students use *Activity Support: Recommendations* to complete the activity. **(Verbal)**

40 min

L1 Special Needs Talk with students about how life on an island would be different from life in the United States, especially for a country trying to make and grow all goods.

---

3 Understand

Review Ask students to use their own reports to identify problems Cuba has faced in the past 50 or so years. Have them try to match the proposed solutions under the heading *Cuba's Future* to these problems.

Assess Have students write their responses to the Assessment questions in their notebooks. Write events from the feature on chart paper and tape them out of order at the front of the room. Ask students to come up and rearrange them, without looking at their books.

Remediate If students struggle to understand the effects of Castro's original plan, create a table with one column titled *What Castro Wanted to Happen* and one titled *What Did Happen*, connected by right-pointing arrows. Have students help you fill in the table with information from the feature.

Name _____ Class _____ Date _____

myWorld Activity Support   **Recommendations**

Report on Cuba

Directions As observers from the United Nations Development
Programme (UNDP), it is your job to report on current conditions in
Cuba. Use information from the Case Study to fill in the table below.
Then use the completed table to list four recommendations.

Category	Current Conditions	UNDP Assistance Needed?
Economic Growth		
Education		
Health		
Foreign Relations		
Personal Freedoms		

The UNDP suggests taking the following four steps in Cuba:

1. _____

2. _____

3. _____

4. _____

BACKGROUND

Ripe for Revolution? In the years between Cuba's independence in 1902 and the overthrow of Batista in 1959, the gap between the country's rich and poor became very obvious. The majority of Cubans, many of whom lived in rural areas, lived in extreme poverty and were unemployed. Approximately 75 percent of land suited for agriculture was owned by U.S. and other foreign investors, and 40 percent of sugar production was controlled by outside parties. During this time, the government was characterized by corrupt elections and equally corrupt officials— circumstances that caused many farmers, students, and young professionals to welcome the nationalist message Fidel Castro began to promote in the early 1950s.

GUIDE ON THE SIDE

Historical Overview

- **Sequence** Name, in chronological order, the countries that governed Cuba from the 1500s to the 1900s. (Spain, the United States, Cuba)

- **Make Inferences** Why do you think so many Americans continued to be involved in Cuba after it became independent? (Some Americans made a lot of money in a country that was just beginning to control itself.)

Analyze Visuals Have students examine both images of Fidel Castro.

- What does the billboard tell you about the feelings of Castro's government toward the revolution? (The government considers the revolution an ongoing event, more than 45 years after Castro started it.)

Case Study

Cuba: Revolution to Today

Key Ideas
- The Cuban Revolution resulted in a communist dictatorship under Fidel Castro.
- Cuba's command economy provides social services but limits economic growth.
- Economic problems may force Cuba to carry out political and economic reforms.

Key Terms • ally   • literacy   • rationing   • embargo

Cuba has been a communist country for more than 50 years. Communism has had mixed results. Although Cubans have good access to healthcare and education, the government limits citizens' rights. The government also keeps strict control of the economy. Cubans cannot freely elect their leaders or criticize the government. Today, however, Cuba is slowly changing as the government allows more economic freedom. Will political freedom follow?

Historical Overview

Spain ruled Cuba for nearly 400 years. Then, in 1898, the United States defeated Spain in the Spanish–American War and took control of Cuba. In 1902 Cuba gained its independence.

The United States kept a strong influence in Cuba after independence. The U.S. government supervised Cuba's economy and its foreign relations. American investors and businesses developed sugar plantations and other industries. By the 1950s, Cuba was one of the

Fidel Castro, below right, took control of Cuba in 1959. ▼

2007
Año 49 de la
REVOLUCIÓN

ANSWERS

PRIMARY SOURCE

In Castro's Words Review Fidel Castro's revolution goals with students. Then read them the following quotations by Castro. Prompt them to consider the quotations first in the context of the years immediately following the overthrow of Batista and then in the context of Cuba today (described on p. 267). Ask, Who do you think is more likely to agree with the first quote, people hearing it in the 1960s or people hearing it today? How does Cuba's economic system compare with the system described in the second quote?

"The revolution is a dictatorship of the exploited against the exploiters."

"I find capitalism repugnant. It is filthy, it is gross, it is alienating . . . because it causes war, hypocrisy and competition."

Levels of Freedom, 2008

KEY
Freedom, 2008

- Free
- Freedom limited
- Not free

Map Skills
This map shows levels of political rights and civil liberties such as religious freedom. How does freedom vary around the world?

GUIDE ON THE SIDE

- **Infer** Think of what you know about the relationship between the United States and the Soviet Union. Why might the United States have disagreed with Cuba's leadership by the 1960s? (The United States would not want its neighbor to be an ally of its enemy, the Soviet Union.)

Map Skills Have students use the map's key to analyze content.

- Where else in the world does a level of freedom similar to that in Cuba exist? (much of northern, southwest, and central Asia; much of Africa)

Communism in Cuba

- **Identify Details** Under communism, over what do citizens have control: property, businesses, or prices? (Citizens cannot control any of these things under communism.)

- **Express an Opinion** Do you think it is healthy for an economy if all people who work are paid equally? Explain. (Sample: No. If everyone is paid equally, there is no need for people to compete and try to improve their skills.)

wealthiest countries in Central America. But a small group of people—including many Americans—controlled much of the wealth. Most Cubans were very poor.

In 1952 Fulgencio [fool HEN see oh] Batista took power as a dictator. Under his rule, gambling and criminal activities flourished. Batista became increasingly unpopular with the Cuban people.

In 1959 Batista was overthrown in a revolution led by Fidel Castro. Castro said that he wanted to reform Cuba and improve conditions for the Cuban people. His ideas inspired many others in Central America. Before long, however, Castro formed a communist dictatorship that limited Cubans' political liberties. Many people fled Cuba for the United States. Cuba became an ally of the Soviet Union. An **ally** is a political or military partner.

Reading Check What kind of government did Fidel Castro form?

Communism in Cuba

Castro created a communist society in Cuba. Under communism, there are no social classes and no private property. Government owns all property and makes all economic decisions.

The Cuban government took control of farms and businesses. The government made all decisions about what products to produce, what prices to charge, and what wages to pay workers.

Castro wanted all Cubans to enjoy a decent standard of living. He wanted to erase the gap between wealthy and poor people. The government set up a system that provided social benefits to all people. All Cubans got free healthcare and free education. As a result, health conditions and literacy improved. **Literacy** is the ability to read and write.

Reading Check How did the Cuban government influence the economy?

READING CHECK Castro formed a communist dictatorship that closely controlled people's freedoms.

READING CHECK The government controlled farms and businesses and made decisions about what products to produce, what prices to charge, and what wages to pay workers.

MAP SKILLS There is much less freedom in the Eastern Hemisphere than in the Western Hemisphere.

GEOGRAPHY

Immigration to the United States Given that Cuba is only 90 miles south of Key West, Florida, it is not surprising that the United States has consistently been home to a sizable Cuban immigrant population. The 1910 U.S. Census showed that 15,133 Cubans were officially living in the United States, with estimates reaching 124,000 around 1959. Over the years, immigration from Cuba has taken place in waves, skyrocketing as the revolutionary government developed in the 1960s and again in the early 1990s, when the Soviet Union collapsed. In 1994, the U.S. government initiated an annual quota of 20,000 for Cuban immigrants. Illegal immigration by boat continues to take place. In 2006, the Pew Hispanic Center reported that in 2004 there were 1.5 million Cubans living in the United States, 913,000 of whom were born on foreign soil and 60 percent of whom are U.S. citizens.

Analyze Visuals Have students review the different comparisons.

- In which ways are Cuba and the United States similar? (literacy rate, life expectancy)

- Imagine that you lived in Cuba. Give an example of how your life would be different than it is in the United States. (Sample: I would probably be just as educated, although perhaps not as informed, since I would not be able to access the Internet easily.)

- Are you surprised that a government that closely controls its citizens' actions would provide high-quality healthcare and education? Explain. (Samples: Yes, I am surprised. People who are well educated might be more likely to identify how their lives could be better and fight for those improvements. No, I am not surprised. If a government believes all of its actions are correct, then it won't think that providing a good education and healthcare is any different.)

Comparing Cuba and the United States

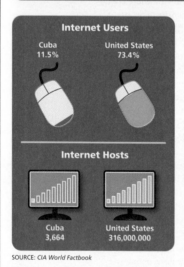

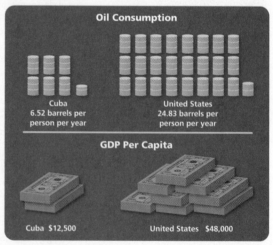

SOURCE: *CIA World Factbook*

READING CHECK Cuba's economy could not produce enough food and goods for its people; it lost aid it had received from other communist countries.

READING CHECK Raúl Castro replaced his brother Fidel as president.

ASSESSMENT 1. Fidel Castro chose to make Cuba a communist country after he took over the government. **2.** The communist government has placed land, most of the economy, and many personal rights under strict government control. It has also ensured that

QUICK FACTS

The Internet in Cuba Despite recent reforms, the Cuban government still maintains tight control over many aspects of its citizens' lives, including access to the Internet and the information obtained through it. Private citizens must have special permission to buy a computer or use the Internet, which has led to black-market sales of illegal passwords and manipulation of the limited public Internet access allowed to tourists. Cuba currently has the lowest rate of Internet use in Latin American, with only two percent of the population capable of connecting to the Internet.

Dream versus Reality

In reality, Castro's communist ideal did not work. Cuba's economy did poorly. The country did not produce enough goods to supply its people. As a result, the government had to set up a rationing system. **Rationing** is the controlled distribution of scarce resources and goods, such as food.

Cuba relied on economic aid from other communist countries, especially the Soviet Union. But those countries had problems too. In 1991 the Soviet Union fell apart. After that, Cuba had even more trouble providing for its people.

As conditions got worse, more Cubans became discontented. Some tried to leave the island. Others began to speak out against the government. But the government cracked down, putting its critics in prison. Many countries criticized Cuba for its lack of rights and freedom.

Reading Check Why did Cuba's economy suffer?

Cuba's Future

In 2008 Fidel Castro's brother, Raúl, became president. Raúl Castro introduced a number of small economic and political reforms. For example, the government removed restrictions against the use of cellphones. It also sought to improve food production by allowing farmers to use some state-owned land.

Better relations with the United States might lead Cuba to become more democratic. For years, the United States has enforced an embargo against Cuba. An **embargo** is the prohibition of trade with a certain country. But in 2009, U.S. President Barack Obama announced that the U.S. government would loosen restrictions on American travel to Cuba. He also signaled U.S. willingness to trade with Cuba if Cuba moves toward democracy and the protection of human rights.

Reading Check What big change occurred in Cuba in 2008?

Because of the U.S. embargo on trade with Cuba, many cars in Cuba date from the 1950s. ▼

GUIDE ON THE SIDE

Dream versus Reality

- **Identify Main Ideas** How did government actions toward critics in the 1990s affect Cuba's foreign relations? (Other countries declared that Cuba was mistreating its citizens.)

Cuba's Future

- **Draw Conclusions** How could the removal of the U.S. embargo help Cubans? (They could trade with the United States for goods they cannot produce.)

Assessment

1. How did Cuba become a communist country?

2. What impact has communism had on Cuba?

3. How does the Cuban government restrict Cubans' actions?

4. How did Cuba change in 2008?

5. Compare and contrast life in Cuba and the United States.

Cubans have a good education and quality healthcare. **3.** The Cuban government does not allow citizens to make decisions about the economy or property. It has also restricted citizens' rights to speak out against government actions. **4.** Under a new president, the government loosened some restrictions on freedoms and economic activity.

5. Sample: In Cuba, people cannot speak out against the government, unlike in the United States. Also, while Americans can be involved in almost all major decisions concerning property and the economy, this type of involvement in Cuba is very limited.

1. Hurricanes and earthquakes are the most common natural disasters in Central America and the Caribbean.

2. The region's warm climate, miles of beaches, and biodiversity make it well suited to tourism.

3. The Maya civilization arose as the result of corn cultivation. The Maya created a system of calendars, a writing system, and city-states.

4. The Spanish set up the encomienda system to control native people. The system resulted in what amounted to slavery for Native Americans, many of whom died from brutal treatment. The system enabled the Spanish to create huge plantations and become wealthy.

5. Before and after independence, Europeans held both wealth and power. Poverty was widespread.

6. The primary roots of Caribbean culture are African. In Central America, they are Native American and Spanish.

7. DR-CAFTA stands for Dominican Republic-Central American Free Trade Association, an agreement that allows free trade among members and reduced taxes on products traded.

THINK CRITICALLY

8. Foreign investors own huge plantations on which they raise food for export and profit. These large plantations limit the amount of land available on which other people can grow their own food.

9. Colonization, encomienda, slavery, independence, dictatorships. The Spanish first colonized the region and then established the encomienda system, which required labor. This system led to the importation of slaves. Later, after the region's countries became independent, many governments became dictatorships.

10. Political corruption and poverty often create instability.

11. Benefits of large-scale agriculture are mainly limited to the amount of profit gained from exporting what is grown. The drawbacks are the use of pesticides and chemical fertilizers, which pollute the region's waters, threaten its ecosystems, and contaminate fishing areas.

Central America and the Caribbean

Chapter Assessment

Key Terms and Ideas

1. **Summarize** What are the different natural disasters that commonly affect Central America and the Caribbean?

2. **Explain** What are the geographic factors of Central America and the Caribbean that make the region well suited for **tourism**?

3. **Describe** Describe how the **Maya** civilization rose and what it accomplished.

4. **Cause and Effect** Why did the Spanish set up the **encomienda** system and what were the results of that system?

5. **Compare and Contrast** How was life in Central America and the Caribbean similar before and after **independence**?

6. **Recall** What are the main roots of Caribbean and Central American culture?

7. **Define** What does DR-CAFTA stand for and what does it allow?

Think Critically

8. **Draw Inferences** What does land ownership have to do with poverty in Central America and the Caribbean today?

9. **Sequence** Put the following terms in chronological order and explain your reasons: dictatorships, colonization, slavery, encomienda, independence.

10. **Draw Conclusions** Why might the leader of a Central American or Caribbean country find it hard to have a stable government?

11. **Core Concepts: Human-Environment Interaction** What are the benefits and drawbacks of large-scale agriculture in Central American and Caribbean countries?

Places to Know

For each place, write the letter from the map that shows its location.

12. Caribbean Sea
13. Lake Atitlán
14. Cuba
15. Costa Rica
16. Lake Nicaragua
17. Dominican Republic
18. **Estimate** Using the scale, estimate the distance between Costa Rica and the Dominican Republic.

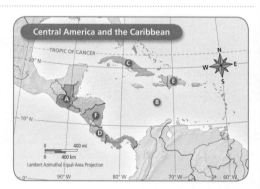

Central America and the Caribbean

---

12. B
13. A
14. C
15. D
16. F
17. E
18. approximately 1,000 miles, or 1,600 kilometers

myWorld Chapter Activity

Venturing in Nicaragua Find Step-by-Step Instructions, Student Instructions and Rubric, and an Activity Support on pp. T33–T35. **(Logical/Visual/Verbal)**

 21st Century Learning

Develop Cultural Awareness Students' questions should be clear and well-thought-out. Answers should include examples that reflect specific aspects of each culture considered.

→ Online Assessment

Tailor review and assessment to each student's needs with an array of online assessments.
- Self-Test
- On Assignment Article or Slideshow
- Success Tracker

? Essential Question

Chapter Transfer Activity

 Venturing in Nicaragua Follow your teacher's instructions to find out more about the different environments, businesses, natural hazards, and opportunities in Nicaragua. Then prepare a plan for a particular kind of tourism business that you will use to seek government or private investment funds.

21st Century Learning

Develop Cultural Awareness

Choose two cultures different from your own that are a part of your community. Then use the Internet or other sources to learn more about these cultures. Write a reflection about how what you learned might change the way you relate to someone of that culture. You might consider researching the following cultural aspects:
- food
- religious practices
- clothing
- gender roles

WRITING TASK TIP

UNDERSTANDING GENRE Before students complete question 3, remind students that radio announcements are extremely brief and rely on words that are spoken to convey a message. Have students practice writing attention-getting "openers" to persuade listeners to conserve fuel or to recycle.

Document-Based Questions

Success **Tracker**
Online at myworldgeography.com

Use your knowledge of Central America and the Caribbean and Documents A and B to answer Questions 1–3.

Document A

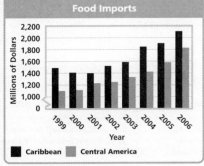

Food Imports

SOURCE: U.S. Department of Agriculture Economic Research Service and U.S. Trade Internet System

1. Which of the following best explains the change shown in Document A?

   A The Caribbean is suffering from a drought.

   B Factory workers are taking jobs on farms.

   C Free-trade laws have made it easier for food to be imported.

   D Foreign food is of better quality than Caribbean or Central American food.

Document B

" You will be engaged in subsistence agriculture in which you will be doing your own small farming ... We need to ensure that our people can feel secured in obtaining not only high quality nutritious food, but it should also be at affordable prices as well ... [Right now] we are importing almost everything that we eat."

—St. Kitts and Nevis Prime Minister Denzil L. Douglas, 2008

2. What slogan would best fit Prime Minister Douglas' new plan for food production?

   A Food Through Trade

   B Back to the Land

   C Worldwide Vegetables

   D Industry Rules

3. **Writing Task** Write a radio announcement persuading people in St. Kitts and Nevis to grow their own vegetables.

DOCUMENT-BASED QUESTIONS

1. C
2. B

3. Students' answers should emphasize the benefits of growing one's own food: increased nutrition and freshness of food, food security, affordability, and lower energy costs.

QUICK FACTS

Resources for Education According to the UNESCO Institute for Statistics, the amount of resources devoted to education varies throughout the Americas.

Guatemala has a pupil-to-teacher ratio of 31 in primary schools. Public spending on education equals 3 percent of the GDP.

Mexico has a pupil-to-teacher ratio of 28 in primary schools. Public spending on education equals

5.5 percent of the GDP.

Belize has a pupil-to-teacher ratio of 23 in primary schools. Public spending on education equals 5.3 percent of the GDP.

The United States has a pupil-to-teacher ratio of 14 in primary schools. Public spending on education equals 5.3 percent of the GDP.

GUIDE ON THE SIDE

21st Century Learning

Solve Problems Ask students what steps they follow when they have to solve a problem. To guide their thinking, write two questions on the board: "How do you analyze the problem?" and "How do you find solutions to the problem?" Record student responses on the board under the appropriate categories. They may say such things as "look for causes" and "ask my friends' advice." Explain that students will work in groups to apply this two-step process to the problem of unemployment in Middle America.

21st Century Learning — Solve Problems

Young and Unemployed in Middle America

Your Mission Study the graphs showing education, literacy, and foreign investment in Belize, Guatemala, and Mexico. Use what you learn to propose a jobs program that helps young people find work in those countries.

In Middle America, the job market is generally weak. Finding a job is even more difficult for young people in this region. They want to work, but they may lack training or transportation. The job market also suffers when business development is slow. Finding a solution to high unemployment rates requires learning more about the factors and circumstances that have led to this situation.

Being young and unemployed in Middle America is part of the problem, but your ideas can be part of the solution.

STEP 1

Identify the Problem.

Employment is desirable not simply because it generates income. Having a job means working toward a goal, learning new skills or information, and improving one's quality of life. Belize, Guatemala, and Mexico are very different nations. They also share certain characteristics. Before you can propose an employment solution, you have to learn more about why people there are unemployed.

STEP 2

Analyze the Data.

As you analyze the graphs, recall what you read in this unit about the geography, history, and current situation in Middle America. How might factors such as education affect unemployment? Do additional research to fill in the gaps in your analysis. You might also find that newspaper articles and photographs provide helpful information about job markets in faraway countries.

STEP 3

Propose a Solution.

Working in groups, prepare a presentation based on one of the graphs provided on the next page. Explain the data in the graph and show how it relates to unemployment in all three subject nations. Integrate what you have learned into your group's final presentation on the proposed government jobs program. Your solution should be flexible enough to work in each nation, given its unique circumstances.

YOUNG AND UNEMPLOYED IN MIDDLE AMERICA RUBRIC
3. Analysis includes an accurate reading of the graph in addition to research online and in the unit. The presentation includes at least three links between the topic of their graph and unemployment among young people. The proposed jobs program addresses the specific cause represented in the graph. The presentation uses evidence such as the graph, photographs, and stories to support the proposed program.

ECONOMY

Composition of the Economy When planning a jobs program, a government can focus on training workers for the existing economic conditions, or it can focus on training workers for the areas where it wants the economy to grow. With either approach, knowing the current composition of the economy can be helpful. In Guatemala, about half of the labor force works in agriculture. Coffee, bananas, and sugar are the main crops. However,

agriculture produces only about one eighth of the nation's income. In Mexico, 59 percent of the laborers work in services, 26 percent in industry, and 15 percent in agriculture. In Belize, 62 percent of laborers work in services, 18 percent in industry, and 20 percent in agriculture.

Go to myWorldGeography.com for help with this activity.

Median Years of Schooling

SOURCE: *CIA World Factbook*

Literacy Rates

SOURCE: *CIA World Factbook*

Foreign Investment

	2005	2006	2007
Guatemala	$508 million	$592 million	$724 million
Mexico	$20.9 billion	$19.3 billion	$24.7 billion
Belize	$127 million	$104 million	$112 million

SOURCE: The World Bank

2. Analysis includes a mostly accurate reading of the graph and some research. The presentation includes 2 links between the graph topic and unemployment. The proposed jobs program somewhat addresses the graph. The presentation uses some evidence to support the proposal.

1. Analysis includes an inaccurate reading of the graph and no research. The presentation includes 1 link between the topic of the graph and unemployment. The proposed jobs program does not address the graph. Presentation uses little evidence to support the proposal.

ANSWERS

GUIDE ON THE SIDE

TakingITGlobal for Educators

Have your students go to myworldgeography.com to find solutions to this 21st Century Learning Activity, *Young and Unemployed in Middle America.*

 21c Online Tutor

Using the 21st Century Online Tutor, students can get more tips on how to analyze and solve problems. Students respond onscreen to successfully learn and apply problem-solving skills.

Mexico

See rubric on p. T6.

myWorld Chapter Activity:
A Time for Judgment

Profile Answers will vary depending on the leader described.

Montezuma II born to royalty; studied to be a warrior and a priest; led Aztec army and expanded empire; defeated by Cortés; strengthened Aztec legacy

Cortés born poor; became a clerk; sought adventure; cultivated Indian allies and defeated Aztecs; distributed encomiendas, which created wealth for a few and poverty for the majority of Mexicans

Maximilian I born to Austrian royalty; served in the military and as a diplomat; as emperor of Mexico, supported freedom of the press, freed peasants in servitude; died in battle

Benito Juárez Native American, born poor; studied to be a priest, became a lawyer; wanted to give land to the poor, separate church and state; became president, led resistance movement that overthrew Maximilian; achieved some reforms; helped liberate Mexico from France's influence

Zapata Mestizo, raised brothers and sisters; supported land reform by negotiation and force; made little progress with land reform; helped overthrow Diaz

Calderón father in politics; became a lawyer and politician, PAN president; elected president of Mexico in 2006; moved against illegal drugs; reformed tax system; supports free enterprise; "modernized" economy

Statement Answers should include a valid reason for the student's choice. Sample: Cortés had the greatest effect on Mexico's history because he conquered the Aztecs and introduced the encomienda system. By distributing large amounts of land to the Spanish, this system left most Mexicans with little or no land and led to widespread poverty.

Section 1
Mexico

myWorld Activity: Mexico Goes Global

Sample:

Location	Resource	Industrial Potential
Gulf Coastal Plain	Oil, natural gas	Petroleum refining
Mexican Plateau	Copper	Electronic components
Pacific Coastal Lowlands	Corn	Food processing

Site Selection Sample: The Pacific Coast is an agricultural region where food processing plants could be set up. The coast offers easy access to shipping.

Enrichment: A Slowly Sinking City

1. Pumping too much water out of the ground is the major cause of subsidence.

2. Sample: Mexico City cannot afford to keep growing because it is already sinking as a result of its large population's demand for water.

Section 1 Quiz

1. d **2.** b **3.** c **4.** b **5.** d

6.

Activity	Environmental Impact
Urban growth	Air pollution
Clear-cutting	Infertile soil
Overgrazing	Land becomes desert

Section 2
Mexico

myWorld Activity: To Dig or Not to Dig

Costs of Destroying the Shopping Mall People would lose their jobs. Businesses would have to relocate or close. Neighborhoods might suffer from the loss of businesses.

Benefits of Digging Up Tenochtitlán Valuable artifacts might be recovered. Archaeological discoveries would aid historians in better understanding the Aztec civilization. Discoveries might increase tourism, thereby contributing to the economy.

Position Statement (My Argument)

For Sample: Shopping malls can always be relocated. Tenochtitlán is a unique historical site. It is important to understand our past.

Against Sample: The dig would unfairly destroy the livelihood of the workers and owners of the businesses within the mall. Business owners might not be fairly compensated or able to relocate. The present is more important than the past.

Enrichment: Maize Makes History

1. Corn was important to early civilizations because it marked the beginning of agriculture. It was the first crop to be cultivated, which meant that people could settle in one place and not have to keep moving to find sources of food.

2. The study of ancient plant remains helps historians understand where people lived.

Section 2 Quiz

1. c   2. d   3. b   4. a   5. c
6. 1519: E; 1810: A; 1821: B; 1910: D; 1917: C

Primary Source: The Struggle Continues

1. Farmers will be unable to sell their corn for the same low price as the imported corn and still make a profit.

2. They blame the Mexican government. Mexican revolutionaries also felt that the government treated farmers unfairly.

Section 3
Mexico

myWorld Activity: Get a Job
Farm Worker

Students choosing this option should include the following points: The farm is fair trade so they are likely to receive a fair wage. There is an opportunity for a good worker to obtain a full-time position. Applicants should like to work outdoors and prefer to work for a local business.

Auto Worker

Students choosing this option should include the following points: The job is full-time. There would be the opportunity to work overtime. Applicants should want to work for a new and/or European company.

Enrichment: Biography of David Alfaro Siqueiros

1. His art honored Mexican workers and drew attention to such issues as safety in the workplace.

2. Sample: After people from other countries viewed Siqueiros's art, they became more aware of similar issues in their own countries.

Section 3 Quiz

1. b   2. c   3. a   4. d   5. b
6. **1999 political reforms** Cause: political unrest. Effect: more open elections; **NAFTA** Cause: desire for increased trade. Effect: increased trade with U.S. and Canada

Case Study: Rise and Fall of the Aztecs

Examples of Aztec Influence

Food use of terracing and irrigation to grow crops; building of islands to create new fields

Artifacts Zocalo, Aztec Stadium, Aztec pyramid

Language Nahuatl words such as *avocado, chili, coyote, chocolate, tomato, ocelot*

Central America and the Caribbean

See rubric on p. T34.

myWorld Chapter Activity: Venturing in Nicaragua

Location	Types of Business
Pacific Coast	Traditional resort, eco-lodge
Managua	Tour agency, museum
Caribbean Coast and Islands	Surf lodge, wildlife tour agency

Selected Location Answers will vary but should include one of the three locations. Sample answer: The Caribbean Coast is a good location for a surf lodge.

Description of Business Answers will vary but should describe one of the three business types. Sample answer: A surf lodge offers surfing lessons, scuba diving, and snorkeling for tourists to explore coral reefs.

Benefits	Risks	Responses to Risks
Scuba rentals attract tourists.	Beginners might feel unsafe.	Teach guests how to use the equipment.
Boat rentals attract tourists.	Residents might complain about noise.	Restrict activities to certain hours.
Nature tours educate tourists.	Crowds could harm the environment.	Hire trained and certified tour guides.
Sell local products; employ residents	Employees might ask for higher wages.	Give employees discounts at local shops.

Section 1
Central America and the Caribbean

myWorld Activity: Location Equation

Grid set answers Sets will vary, but should demonstrate knowledge of Section 1. Sample grid set: location: tropical rain forest; land use: banana or sugar plantation; natural disaster: hurricane

1. Sample answer: These characteristics are typical of a Caribbean region, as the rain forest climate allows for crop growth, but hurricanes are common and could destroy the crops.

2. Sample answer: A hurricane could devastate the economy because flooding and strong winds could destroy homes, businesses, and crops.

Enrichment: Earthquakes in El Salvador

1. The 7.7 earthquake on January 13, 2001, had the greatest magnitude.

2. Two earthquakes in 2001 caused the greatest loss of life. An earthquake with the lowest magnitude can still cause the most deaths if it occurs in a heavily populated area with badly constructed apartments.

Section 1 Quiz

1. d **2.** a **3.** b **4.** a **5.** b
6.

Cause	Effect on Environment
Cattle ranching	Erosion
Tourism	Population density, water shortages
Deforestation	Poor soil, erosion, decline in wildlife

Section 2
Central America and the Caribbean

myWorld Activity: Corners of History
Early Maya (A.D. 250–900)

The economy was based on agriculture and trade. Natural resources were protected. Local people controlled the wealth.

Colonialism (1492 to 1821)

The economy was based on agriculture and trade. Slavery was present. Few people owned land. Foreign influence was strong.

Early Independence (1821 to 1870)

The economy was based on agriculture and trade. Few people owned land. Foreign influence was strong.

Foreign Involvement (1870 to present)

The economy was based on agriculture and trade. Foreign influence was strong.

Reflection

Samples: The statement "Natural resources were protected," and the statement "Local people controlled the wealth," apply only to the early Maya. "Natural resources were protected" only applies to the early Maya because after that era, people began to mine gold and other natural resources. After independence, American economic influence grew, but democracy did not. Few people owned land before and after independence, and foreign influence remained strong.

Enrichment: Maya Math

1. a shell, a dot, and a bar

2. Replace the value at the bottom with three bars.

Section 2 Quiz

1. b   2. d   3. c   4. a   5. b
6.

Encomienda system It became a brutal system of slavery without religious teaching in which enslaved Africans replaced Native American laborers.
Slavery Many native people died from disease or abuse, so enslaved Africans were imported by the Spanish and by sugar planters. Slavery became part of the triangular trade system, making European colony rulers wealthy.
Foreign investment In the Caribbean, U.S. investors controlled industries and land in Panama. They built plantations and the Panama Canal, increasing trade.

Primary Source: The Maya

myWorld Activity: *Popol Vuh* for Kids

Storyboards and books will vary but should demonstrate an understanding of "The Maya" and facts on this page. For example, text should explain that the Maya built pyramid-shaped temples and great city-states, grew corn and other crops, and worshiped many gods. Illustrations might include colored drawings of corn, and perhaps a human sprouting from a corn husk to depict the creation story from the *Popol Vuh*.

Section 3
Central America and the Caribbean

myWorld Activity: Is Free Fair?

1. Sample: Brazilian, Korean, and U.S. companies will invest in Central American businesses.

2. Sample: Mr. Solis believes that free trade helps wealthy countries, or "big beasts," more than the poor country of Costa Rica, a "small beast."

Reasons to Oppose CAFTA

Free trade may help wealthy countries more than poor countries. Pesticides and fertilizer used by farmers can harm the environment. Most farmers don't profit from international trade.

Reasons to Support CAFTA

Low taxes can encourage foreign businesses to build factories, creating jobs. Free trade can help to increase manufacturing.

Enrichment: Microcredit—Helping to Reduce Poverty

1. Dieula was eligible because she was a poor resident of the Dominican Republic who needed help starting and expanding her own business.

2. Sample: The Esperanza loan program is successful because it helps people in poor countries start and expand businesses, which helps the economy.

Section 3 Quiz

1. c   **2.** d   **3.** c   **4.** a   **5.** b

6.

Positive Effect	Group	Negative Effect
They may get microcredit to start their own farms.	Farmers	Free trade may increase competition.
Low taxes help create factories and jobs.	Factory workers	Wages may be lower than with fair trade.
Free trade increases their wealth.	Foreign investors	Only wealthy countries are likely to benefit.

Case Study: Cuba: Revolution to Today

myWorld Activity: Report on Cuba

Answers in order of Category, Current Conditions, and UNDP Assistance Needed?

Economic Growth Raúl Castro's reforms may help the economy. Sample answer: Yes

Education Free education has increased literacy. Sample answer: Yes

Health Free healthcare has improved health conditions. Sample answer: Yes

Foreign Relations Cuba has good relations with some countries. Sample answer: Yes

Personal Freedoms Cuba is still a dictatorship, but Raúl Castro has introduced reforms that increase personal freedoms. Sample answer: Yes

We recommend that the UNDP suggest taking the following four steps in Cuba:

1. Support Raúl Castro's reforms that make the country more democratic and help Cubans prosper.

2. Encourage programs to increase political freedom.

3. Assist the government in providing better healthcare for the poor.

4. Work to improve U.S. relations with Cuba.

Acknowledgments

The people who made up the **myWorld Geography** team—representing composition services; core design, digital, and multimedia production services; digital product development; editorial; editorial services; materials management; and production management—are listed below.

Leann Davis Alspaugh, Sarah Aubry, Deanna Babikian, Paul Blankman, Alyssa Boehm, Peter Brooks, Susan Brorein, Megan Burnett, Todd Christy, Neville Cole, Bob Craton, Michael Di Maria, Glenn Diedrich, Frederick Fellows, Jorgensen Fernandez, Thomas Ferreira, Patricia Fromkin, Andrea Golden, Mary Ann Gundersen, Christopher Harris, Susan Hersch, Paul Hughes, Judie Jozokos, John Kingston, Kate Koch, Stephanie Krol, Karen Lepri, Ann-Michelle Levangie, Salena LiBritz, Courtney Markham, Constance J. McCarty, Laurie McKenna, Anne McLaughlin, Rich McMahon, Mark O'Malley, Alison Muff, Jen Paley, Gabriela Perez Fiato, Judith Pinkham, Paul Ramos, Charlene Rimsa, Marcy Rose, Rashid Ross, Alexandra Sherman, Owen Shows, Melissa Shustyk, Jewel Simmons, Ted Smykal, Emily Soltanoff, Frank Tangredi, Simon Tuchman, Elizabeth Tustian, Merle Uuesoo, Alwyn Velasquez, Andrew White, Heather Wright

Maps

XNR Productions, Inc.

Illustration

Kerry Cashman, Marcos Chin, Dave Cockburn, Jeremy Mohler

Note: T page numbers below refer to teacher resource pages. Other page numbers refer to Western Hemisphere Student Edition pages.

Photography

TABLE OF CONTENTS: Pages vi–vii, All, Pearson Education, Inc.

MIDDLE AMERICA REGIONAL OVERVIEW: Pages 200–205 Bkgrnd sky, ImageSource/Getty Images; **Page 201, LM,** Pearson Education, Inc.; **RM,** Pearson Education, Inc.; **Bkgrnd,** Gary718/Shutterstock; **202, LB,** Michael Boyny/age Fotostock; **LT,** Robert Francis/Photolibrary; **RB,** Dreamtours/Photolibrary; **203, LT,** Sébastien Boisse/Photononstop/Photolibrary; **204, LM,** Susana Gonzalez/Newsmakers/Getty Images; **LB,** Brian Bailey/Getty Images; **RM,** Richard Bickel/Corbis; **RB,** Andoni Canela/Photolibrary; **205, L,** Pearson Education, Inc.; **R,** Pearson Education, Inc.

MEXICO: Pages 206–209, All, Pearson Education, Inc.; **210, Bkgrnd,** Travel Ink/Alamy; **B,** Robert Fried/Alamy; **212, LT,** Scott S. Warren/National Geographic Stock; **LB,** Ales Liska/Shutterstock; **RB,** LOOK Die Bildagentur der Fotografen GmbH/Alamy; **RT,** Radius Images/Alamy; **213, RT,** Didier Dorval/Radius Images/Jupiter Images; **RB,** urosr/Shutterstock; **LB,** Geoff Dann/Dorling Kindersley; **RM,** Rusty Dodson/Shutterstock; **215, RM,** Richard Melloul/Sygma/Corbis; **217, R,** AFP Photo/Jorge Uzon/Newscom; **222, LB,** The Trustees of The British Museum/Art Resource, NY; **223, T,** Demetrio Carrasco/Conaculta-Inah-Mex. Authorized reproduction by the Instituto Nacional de Antropología e Historia/Dorling Kindersley; **M,** The Granger Collection, New York; **B,** The Granger Collection, New York; **224,** The Art Archive/National Palace Mexico City/Gianni Dagli Orti; **R,** The Art Archive/National Palace Mexico City/Gianni Dagli Ort; **225, L,** The Art Archive/National Palace Mexico City/Alfredo Dagli Orti; **226,** Schalkwijk/Art Resource, NY; **227, L,** The Art Archive/National Palace Mexico City/Gianni Dagli Orti; **R,** Schalkwijk/Art Resource, NY; **230,** Jeff Topping/Reuters; **231, LB,** Library of Congress; **BM,** AFP/Getty Images; **RB,** Jorge Silva/Reuters; **RM,** Holger Mette/Shutterstock; **218,** Peter Wilson/Conaculta-Inah-Mex. Authorized reproduction by the Instituto Nacional de Antropología e Historia/Dorling Kindersley; **219, B,** Ken Welsh/age Fotostock; **220, T,** The Art Archive/Museo Ciudad Mexico/Gianni Dagli Orti; **B,** Agencia el Universal/Newscom; **221, T,** Glowimages RF/age Fotostock; **B,** Holger Mette/Shutterstock; **228, RB,** Bettmann/Corbis; **RT,** David Crossland/Alamy; **229, RB,** Adam Woolfitt/Corbis; **232, LB,** L. Zacharie/Alamy; **RB,** Danny Lehman/Corbis; **232–233,** Peregrina/iStockphoto.com; **233, LB,** Robert Harding Picture Library/age Fotostock; **RB,** Andy Mead/Icon SMI/Newscom; **234, L,** Linda Whitwam/Dorling Kindersley; **235,** AP Photo/Carlos Osorio; **236, LB,** Paul E. Rodriguez/Newscom; **BM,** Keith Dannemiller/Alamy; **LT,** Ivan Vdovin/age Fotostock; **RT,** Ivan Vdovin/age Fotostock.

CENTRAL AMERICA AND THE CARIBBEAN: Pages 240–243, All, Pearson Education, Inc.; **244, RB,** Frans Lemmens/zefa/Corbis; **Bkgrnd,** P. Narayan/age Fotostock; **246, LT,** Jeff Grabert/Shutterstock, Inc.; **RT,** Demetrio Carrasco/JAI/Corbis; **RM,** Stephen Frink/Corbis; **RB,** Radius Images/Alamy; **247,** Jeff Greenberg/PhotoEdit; **249,** John Miller/Robert Harding World Imagery/Corbis; **250, B,** Enrique de la Osa/Reuters; **251,** Lynn M. Stone/Nature Picture Library; **252, L,** Jim Clare/Nature Picture Library; **LB,** The Art Archive/Archaeological Museum Tikal Guatemala/Gianni Dagli Orti; **253, RT,** The Granger Collection, New York; **RB,** The Art Archive; **254,** Time & Life Pictures/Getty Images; **255,** AP/Wide World Photo; **256, T,** The Art Archive/National Anthropological Museum Mexico/Gianni Dagli Orti; **B,** John Elk III/Alamy; **257, T,** I. Kolesnik/Shutterstock; **B,** The Print Collector/Alamy; **258,** Laurent Grandadam/age Fotostock; **259, L,** Owen Franken/Corbis; **LM,** www.imagesource.com/Newscom; **R,** Pearson Education, Inc.; **RM,** Holly Wilmeth/Aurora Photos/Corbis; **RT,** AP Images; **T,** Sharon Hudson/Corbis; **260,** Mark Edwards/Still Pictures/Peter Arnold, Inc.; **261,** Didi/Alamy; **262, T,** Pearson Education, Inc.; **263, RB,** Pearson Education, Inc.; **264, L,** Corbis; **264, R,** Alvaro Leiva/age Fotostock; **267,** Reinhard Rohner/age Fotostock.

MIDDLE AMERICA UNIT CLOSER: Page 270, iStockphoto; **271,** Pearson Education, Inc.

Text

Grateful acknowledgment is made to the following for copyrighted material:

Page T23 The New York Times
"Mexican Farmers Protest End of Corn-Import Taxes" by James C McKinley Jr. from *The New York Times, February 1, 2008.* All rights reserved. Used by permission and protected by the Copyright Laws of the United States. The printing, copying, redistribution, or retransmission of the material without express permission is prohibited.

Note: Every effort has been made to locate the copyright owner of material reproduced in this publication. Omissions brought to our attention will be corrected in subsequent editions.